60
Art Projects
for Children

60
Art Projects for Children

Painting, Clay, Puppets,
Prints, Masks, and More

Jeannette Mahan Baumgardner

Clarkson Potter/Publishers
New York

The publisher gratefully acknowledges permission to reprint from *Here They Come: Ready or Not! A Report of the School Readiness Task Force*, copyright © 1988 California State Department of Education, PO Box 271, Sacramento, CA 95802-0271.

Published by Clarkson N. Potter Inc., 201 East 50th Street, New York, New York 10022. Member of the Crown Publishing Group.

Random House, Inc. New York, Toronto, London, Sydney, Auckland

CLARKSON N. POTTER, POTTER, and colophon are trademarks of Clarkson N. Potter, Inc.

Manufactured in the United States of America

Design by Renato Stanisic

Library of Congress Cataloging-in-Publication Data
Baumgardner, Jeannette Mahan.
   60 art projects for children / Jeannette Mahan Baumgardner.
   Includes bibliographical references (p. 110) and index.
   1. Art—Study and teaching (Elementary)—United States—Handbooks, manuals, etc. 2. Project method in teaching. I. Title.
N362.B38   1993
372.5′044—dc20
                                       92-17164
                                          CIP
                                          AC

ISBN 0-517-88008-3

10 9 8 7 6 5 4 3 2

To the memory of
Lupine Zdzienicka Fanshel
October 7, 1975–April 30, 1991

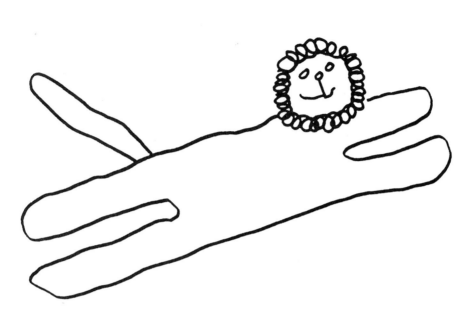

This book is for those who believe that children want to be challenged and, when encouraged, have a drive to overcome obstacles with concentration and energy.

This book is for parents and teachers who have enough assistance to work with children in groups of about seven. There are also some projects suitable for public school–sized class groups. A compilation of twenty years of experience with children and art, this book contains projects from many sources. They have all been refined by many hands, large and small, in the last nine years of The Summertime Arts & Crafts Workshop, Sebastopol, California.

ACKNOWLEDGMENTS

This book was made possible by the enthusiasm and support of many people who gave freely of themselves, and I am indebted to them all:

Alice Smith, for her wisdom, constant encouragement, and gracious assistance in every aspect of this project

Richard Frank, treasurer; David Smith, president; and all the other members of the board of the Smith Family Foundation, for their faith and trust

Carol McNeill, for her faith in me and in this book, and her generous help in getting it off the ground

Nora Fanshel, for her enrichment of the art projects themselves, her comments and additions to this book, and her example of commitment to integrity in life and art

Rita Sever, for her interviews with the children of the Open Alternative School, Sebastopol, California, to obtain their own words about their art; for her assistance in the classroom, and with fundraising and registration; and for her sustaining enthusiasm

Janet Jenkins, for her contributions to the weaving and spinning projects and for her continuing, unfailing support

Mike McBride, for his wonderful photographs, which illustrate this book; for creating and sustaining the Open Alternative School, in which I was able to develop many of these projects; and for being my master teacher there and providing the model for The Summertime Arts & Crafts Workshop

Linda Merryman, for her work in creating a video diary of the workshop, and for her ongoing support as a parent in the program

Hal Sunderland, whose advice and encouragement was in large part responsible for the creation of the workshop

Candace Demeduc, for her patient and congenial editing of my original manuscript

Cathy Jo Vozobule, for her fine photographic contributions to this book

Helen Gin, who has assisted in numerous ways both large and small over the years

Jean Mann, for generously sharing her thoughtful suggestions and proofreading skills, and Carol Middleton, for her helpful comments and questions during the rough-draft stage of this book

The businesses and service clubs of Sebastopol, California; the City of Sebastapol; Mel Davis, city manager; and the Parks & Recreation commissioners, headed by Greg Jacobs, for continued support of the workshops

The parent volunteers who worked with me in class and out

The children who love art and provide my continuing education

Finally, to my family—my sons, Joel and Will, inspirations both, for moving the heavy stuff, laying floors, putting up Sheetrock and shelves, assisting in class, having their telephone taken over during the early years of the workshop, and (more recently) teaching me how to operate a computer so this book could be published; and my husband, Frank, for much of the above and for his constant love and support, which makes all possible.

CONTENTS

INTRODUCTION

Creation Myth of the Uitoto People of Colombia

Nothing existed, not even a stick to support the vision; our Father attached the illusion to the thread of a dream and kept it by the aid of his breath. He sounded to reach the bottom of the appearances, because there was nothing. Nothing existed indeed.

Then the Father again investigated the bottom of the mystery. He tied the empty illusion to the dream thread and pressed the magical substances upon it. Thus, by the aid of the dream, he held it like a wisp of raw cotton.

—as passed on to me by Janet Jenkins, as passed on to her by a teacher

I saw a photograph years ago in a book whose title I can't remember. The image returns to me periodically because it stirred in me a powerful realization about children, adults, culture, society, and learning. Five or six South American women were sitting around a fountain in a dusty courtyard, weaving. In between them were two or three children, learning how to weave by imitating the women. It dawned on me that this was wonderful and true—a few children learning by doing at their mothers' or aunts' or neighbors' elbows, learning because they were to become part of an adult society.

Most North American children are placed in a classroom where one lone adult is trying to help as many as thirty children. And when our children do get to put their hands on things, they are often fake things. Plastic vacuum cleaners with little plastic beads spinning around uselessly, or plastic lawn mowers that can't cut a wet noodle. We all, including the children, know the deception involved and what it implies. Obviously, I wouldn't give a child a real lawn mower to work with. But, there are many authentic materials and tools with which children can work safely and effectively.

In the United States we are becoming more and more removed from the processes that turn raw materials into products, and even from the raw materials themselves. Time, the greatest stuff of children's lives, is taken up with activities and prod-ucts that have been so processed, refined, de-spirited, and removed from their origins that they themselves are lifeless. Children are in danger of becoming customers in life rather than participants, consumers rather than producers. As a result, children don't know the sources of basic materials, what the materials looked like before they were processed, or how the finished products were made. If they live in the country, the children might have a better chance at figuring things out for themselves by watching nature at work. If they're lucky, they might see a film about how things are made, and be as excited with this knowledge as was my son, who ran home from school years ago to dig up our back-yard to make adobe bricks (he's now studying to be an architect). But, in general, children don't have the opportunity to use real tools or real materials, and they are ignorant of the equally important processes involved.

Of the several hundreds of children I've worked with, I can safely say that the one thing they all have in common is the palpitating desire to participate. They want to do things that adults do, use things that adults use, get results that adults get. Adults don't use fake tools, they don't make useless or at least purposeless things, and they don't sim-ulate doing jobs. Playing "pretend" is an important part of childhood—make-believe allows children to test their identities and social roles. Dealing with

Spinning and weaving teacher Janet Jenkins (center) and company

the physical world is another story. Hands-on activity cannot be faked if sensory development, mature judgment, and self-esteem are to bloom.

Like the materials and processes of everyday life, art also has become removed from people, turned over to the "experts." Fine art is now confined to museums. These institutions mount spectacular shows for which we must purchase tickets in advance and see in crowded, snaking lines behind ropes and electric eyes. To the few children who actually do see these shows, the message is that art doesn't belong in real life; it is something to visit once in a while. Much contemporary art is unintelligible to people, and, as a result, intimidating. This distance from making is worsened by the fact that our everyday objects are machine-made. We are not a society that grows and harvests straw, then dries and weaves it. No soul shines through our mass-produced ceramic mugs and plastic figurines. Our holiday art is a printed greeting card or paper decoration; when we buy something handmade, most often it is from some other country. Though art does indeed play a major role in our everyday lives, the average person thinks it is something they know nothing about. We have trouble making a connection between the designs and structures that surround us and a human being–artist.

So, how do we get art back in our lives? How do we respond to the desperate need to develop creativity in our children? For someone just beginning this quest, art projects may seem overwhelming. Just assembling the materials looks difficult in these days when art-supply stores cater to commercial artists and carry expensive lines of fine-art supplies and "craft" stores are stocked with predesigned, ready-to-assemble kits. All it really takes is the desire to begin and a little practical guidance.

I hope this book will fill the need for practical information that will inspire the young and the old, and that the combined experience of the teachers and students at The Summertime Arts & Crafts Workshop will help those wishing to bring art into the lives of children.

We don't need to give up progress in order to continue the traditions of handcrafts from the past. We do need to integrate these traditions, along with the gains of progress, into the lives of children. Only then can we forge a culture out of the best of the past and the best of the present. Along the way, we will give the children the chance to know what it's like to make a positive impact, to realize they are creators. As Rudolph Arnheim said: "A genuine culture depends less on the rare geniuses than the creative life of the average citizen."

THE VALUE OF ART FOR CHILDREN

WHAT I HAVE LEARNED OVER THE YEARS

Children must be given the opportunity to make choices and decisions for themselves, or their lives as adults will be much more difficult than they should be. Indecision and lack of self-confidence are made, not born. Art provides the perfect opportunity for young people to exercise their own ideas and judgment in a structured environment and to

Annual exhibit of children's art from the Summertime Arts & Crafts Workshop

reap the additional benefits of working directly with real materials. Art materials have their limits and they speak silently to the student in continuous feedback. Clay is the teacher when it collapses under heavy hands, or paint, when colors turn to mud.

The discovery of how to control clay or paint will often incorporate the happy accident. The physical experience involved when children or adults make art interplays with conscious modifications of technique, forming a continuous loop. Since prehistory, the human brain has developed from just such stimulation. Tools were invented after experiments with rocks. Using a material inspired an idea. Young people must interact directly with the physical world and learn through all their senses, not just those of sight and sound. They must touch and do. Classroom learning needs to be balanced with learning by doing, and "computer" learning needs to be balanced with learning by direct physical contact. As *Here They Come: Ready or Not!*, a report focusing on four- to six-year-olds that was published by the California State Department of Education, states: "Children are motivated by their own desire to make sense of their world."

Young people must have the time and space to explore, create, destroy, accrue, and develop. Children should have the opportunity to try new things and to succeed from a young age. As early as age 10, a child has developed either the ability for self-forgiveness or the fear of failure, the will to open to life or the fear of the world. Some parents have told me that their children have achieved one of their few successes ever at The Summertime Arts & Crafts Workshop, a nonprofit children's art program which I developed and taught in Sebastapol, California. That the workshop contributed to a child's single triumph makes me happy . . . but what a sad reality!

When doing art with children, be sensitive to the

infinite variety of the young people. Do not make the mistake of pre-judging, pre-planning, or predicting what children are. For all their conformity, their devotion to copying and imitating, their dependence on example, and their thirst for someone to show them the way, each child is one-of-a-kind being. Some will force the issue of individual personality; others will never try. The decision making that is crucial to every step of the creative process offers a constructive opportunity for a child to exert his or her unique personality. Decision making is also a basic and crucial life skill, and practicing it in the context of an art project will help a young person become a capable, confident adult. You will find also that art is an activity that clearly demonstrates individual learning needs and styles. It's possible to identify specific areas of physical or emotional disability, as well as strengths, which often go unrecognized in a 3-R curriculum.

Here are a few points to remember:

● Always test new projects on your own before doing them with children. The ideal teacher is one who has passion for his or her work and wants to share it with others. It has been a great advantage to me to go from working in my studio to assisting young people in making art. Moving back and forth this way has kept me honest.

● Resist the urge to prefabricate the projects. If the children aren't involved from start to finish, most of the point will be lost. Think of yourself as a facilitator rather than a teacher. You are bringing together young people, art materials, time, and space.

● Familiarize yourself with as much art as possible. In this book I will mention a few artists to whose work you might refer, but they are by no means a complete or even representative group. Explore your local public and university libraries, museums, galleries, shops, and art festivals. You will have to trust your own judgment in guiding children in art. This may be difficult if you are not familiar with a wide range of work. Approach each child (and art in general) with an open heart and mind. There will be some children who—too swiftly, it may seem—

will turn out beautiful work, loose gestural statements with the kind of spontaneity that older artists dream of. Others may be just plain sloppy. Still others will labor under the onus of an already dictatorial perfectionism. Honest efforts should always be applauded, even if they do not suit your taste. They are just that: efforts. As teachers, our main concern is the effort—the persistence, the care, and the concentration that the child puts into his or her work. I never compare work or have competitions.

● Do not underestimate the power of commercial imagery and how it combines with the life-as-observer-rather-than-participant trend that is dulling our lives. Promote personal imagery whenever you can. Use positive reinforcement to elicit each child's own spirit. If children are constantly told what to do, they will lose touch with their particular spirit and thus be more susceptible to being molded by outside forces. Not all of these forces are benign.

● *Art is not just a leisure-time activity.* It is an essential ingredient to living a human life. As we head toward the twenty-first century, our mainstream culture lacks a spiritual base and ritual system like those that sustained people in the past. Art can be a healing force especially for children because it redirects destructive energy into creative impulses and builds a sense of self-worth that is the foundation of spiritual citizenship. It can produce a meditative state that in itself is a therapeutic balance to the clamor of our world. It cuts across time, space, and cultures to assist in our understanding of global interdependence. It taps into what Carl Jung called the collective unconscious, and through symbols, it connects us to each other and the greater universe. Art for children is not an extra. In the words of Dr. Thomas Armstrong, educational consultant and author: "Children must be allowed to experience their own perceptions and not someone else's expectations for how they are to perceive—in order to fully realize their own true potential. . . . Artistic expression opens the heart to new learning, allowing children to gain control over their feelings and letting them transform strong emotions into new and creative energies."

BASICS

WORK SPACE

Children are accepting and will try to work in any environment. As teachers, we need to make them aware that well-planned, well-organized working conditions will help them achieve the results they want. A work space should be comfortable, with plenty of elbowroom and good light. If your work space is lighted by fluorescent tubes, make sure they are the full-spectrum type so that you will be able to see all colors. Standard fluorescent lights eliminate certain hues, and there is some evidence that these lights are not healthful. Make sure children's work is not too far from their reach or hanging off the edge of the table. If working in a group, see that the students space themselves out. A large "place mat"—a piece of heavy paper or a piece of vinyl—for each child helps define each artist's territory. Arrange materials so that the children don't have to reach across their own or another's work.

Invite the children to inspect all the materials you have provided and to take part in deciding what they will use. Each child should be able to make a statement like this: "I am painting with red because I chose it, not just because it was closest to my hand."

LABELS FOR FINISHED WORK

When working with a group, always make sure to label each child's work with his or her name, not just his or her initials. Even though the students may vehemently assure you they will know their own work, at least half won't recognize it later, especially if it has been transformed by drying or some other process.

Our mixed-age workshop allows sisters and brothers to attend together, creating a natural, familylike atmosphere as part of our basic workspace.

MATERIALS AND EQUIPMENT FOR AN ART PROGRAM

The list that follows in this section cites the items you are likely to need to present a full art program for children. (A specific list for each project will appear with each project description, in chapters to come.) In some instances, these individual lists include brand-name materials of good quality as of this writing. Most of these materials are provided at public schools. Many of them can be gathered from around the house. A few are available only at dealers specializing in them.

Since 1987, California has prohibited the purchase of toxic art supplies for kindergarten through sixth grade and restricted their use for grades seven through twelve. The law is one of voluntary compliance and applies to public and private schools. It is meant to be both a safety guide and a protection against law suits. Most states have guidelines about what art materials are safe to use with kindergarten through sixth-grade children. California and Massachusetts are the most stringent. You may wish to contact your state department of education to learn about these laws of voluntary compliance. We certainly do not want to endanger our children. At the same time, some of the approved products are of inferior quality and very unsatisfactory aesthetically. Try to become as knowledgeable about the hazards of art materials as you can. If you are using a product whose only danger is from ingestion and you are working at home with your own child under very controlled circumstances, you may decide that you can keep your child from eating his or her lump of clay. Some of the banned materials are key ingredients in making the quality art materials that we have come to expect. It is hoped that individual manufacturers can come up with new formulas for

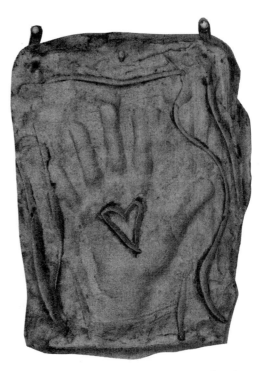

Plaster cast: a traditional school project treated with new creativity by Rosalie Fanshel at age eight.

products that will be equally acceptable. Just because products are for use by children doesn't mean it's okay to sacrifice aesthetic values.

MATERIALS

- Tempera paint
- Acrylic paint
- Oil pastels
- Crayons
- Regular and colored pencils
- Erasers
- Felt-tip pens, permanent and nonpermanent markers of various sizes
- White glue
- Clay
- Glazes for clay
- Plaster of paris
- Paper: Newsprint or other drawing paper, at least 8½ by 11 inches to as large as possible; construction paper; colored tissue; scrap paper of all kinds, such as wrapping paper
- Papier-mâché paste (wallpaper paste) or flour (see page 60–64)
- Masking tape
- Assorted yarns
- Threads, buttons, lace and other trims, beads, etc.
- Fiberfill
- Fishing line
- Scrap wood
- Cardboard pieces and boxes
- Fabric scraps
- Paper bags
- Paper towels
- Soap

EQUIPMENT Paintbrushes: ¼-, ½-, and 1-inch–wide bristle brushes; various sizes of soft brushes for ceramic glazing; glue brushes (stiff bristles); assorted small brushes for detailing; Japanese calligraphy brushes

Assorted clay tools

Assorted scissors, including fabric scissors of high quality

Assorted needles

Pins

Crochet hooks

Clothesline

Clothespins

Large and small containers with lids

Sponges

Exacto knife

Soft brayers

Hammer

Rulers

Pliers

Wire cutter

Mixing spoons

Knives

Plastic buckets

Plastic bowls

Paper clips

Pushpins

Electrical devices: Frying pan, iron, sewing machine

Furniture: At least one, large, smooth-topped work table; bookcase or cabinet to store supplies; wall to display artwork

Optional: Kiln, copy machine

Monoprint by Rosalie Fanshel

DRAWING

TIME As much as possible

MATERIALS Drawing tools: A variety of drawing pencils; Pink Pearl erasers; large, soft colored pencil sets; felt-tip pen sets of different point sizes; an assortment of colored chalk; and oil pastels. For children over 10, provide pastels and vine charcoal to be used with kneaded erasers and small pieces of leather chamois.

Drawing boards: Masonite sheets at least 18 by 24 inches, with pins or clips to hold paper

Paper: A variety of sizes and textures, including slick paper and tracing paper. (Excess computer paper is easily acquired.)

Sketch diaries (spiral-bound tablets), one per child

DOING IT Drawing is a major developmental activity in the lives of children. Allowing your children to draw as much as possible will cultivate a love of learning. Miriam Lindstrom, former curator at the De Young Museum in San Francisco and founder of the museum's visual education program for people of all ages, wrote: "Art demonstrates the truth of diversity and multiple possibility open to the inquiring human spirit."

It's easy to understand why it is harmful for an adult to repeatedly interrupt a child's verbal expression with criticisms and corrections about style and grammar. Repeatedly interrupting to correct a child's drawing is just as destructive. Drawing is the easiest available medium for parents and teachers to provide. A most successful approach is that of my teacher and friend Mike McBride, who, almost daily, provides an "open art" period in which small groups of six or seven create artwork on their own

for up to 30 minutes. Children work individually and together on projects and socialize quietly. The makeup of each group changes from week to week, discouraging competition and comparison.

For young children, simply provide the materials, a supportive work space, and your approval. Encourage diversity. Even some very young people show remarkable sophistication of expression, as the illustration on page 16 shows. At age six, Brendan, the creator of this work, shows a variety of distinctly identifiable animals. He uses overlapping to create a sense of depth. The leopard is in front of the grass; the grass in front of the elephant, who is in front of the tree, which is in front of a mountain. The snake coiled around the tree branch disappears behind the branch and wraps around in front of it. The zebras in the distance are quite small compared to the animals in the foreground, showing that Brendan has a surprising sense of scale for one

so young. But in another drawing by Brendan, which appears on page 17, the dinosaur, tree, and volcano are all the same size and the same distance from the viewer. The drawing does not distinguish foreground and background. If one child varies so much in his own work, why would we expect or wish for different children to produce similar work?

Young children create wonderful expressions from imagination and memory. But, after the age of about seven, they tend to become critical of their earlier efforts and to use stereotypes for security. The businesses in our society, to a great extent, rely on visual stereotypes. Because children naturally long to be part of society, they use these overworked images as an entrée to it. Remember the happy face? Pac-Man? At about age seven, children are particularly susceptible to the deadening of the imagination that clichéd art projects can cause. However, do not forbid them to use the stereotype of choice, no matter how banal (the images change from year to year). Limiting the children's range of choices undermines them as individuals and as artists. We must offer children many choices and, most important, plenty of drawing experience at a young

age. (If they haven't had this, do your best to let them catch up, and offer plenty of encouragement.)

Sometimes the only way to encourage children to stretch their imaginations and skills is to show them something better than the commercial imagery that surrounds them. Resource material is available as slides, in books, and from museums. When they attempt something unique, your genuine enthusiasm is the best encouragement of all. Children do vary in their need for the security of stereotypes. Having them work in a group can inspire its members if one of them is willing to be daring.

The passion for wanting to make drawings look "real" hits at around 10 years. At this point, young people become dissatisfied and frustrated with their drawing. They have come through an intense period in which they have learned symbols; now the students must set these aside to see what things really look like—the prerequisite of realistic drawing. They have an intense need to make work that looks the same as their neighbors'. Be patient during this time, when the wildly original work of previous years can give way to the most conventional imagery. In responding to their need to make things look real, we can give children plenty of guidance concerning specific drawing skills.

REALISTIC DRAWING SKILLS

To draw realistically, an artist must develop techniques in regard to space and volume, foreshortening, overlapping, perspective, light and shade, proportion, scale, and negative space. Each of these facets of drawing can be explored in simple exercises, demonstrated in the work of artists of other ages and cultures, discussed with students, and practiced for a lifetime.

Words of caution: Because it is a study of visual relationships, drawing is a complex subject. Lindstrom said that learning to draw is like learning to read and write simultaneously. One is observing and recording three-dimensional data and, at the same time, recording and interpreting it in a two-dimensional form. Teachers: Be patient. Like reading, this skill is mastered at different rates by different individuals.

The remainder of this section will discuss each of the aspects of realistic drawing in turn.

Space and volume: To represent three-dimensional objects on the two-dimensional surface of the picture plane, we have to let go of the idea of how they are actually formed. We may know that our house has four walls of equal length that support a level roof. But when we see the house from the driveway, we see three walls at most, and they appear to be different heights. To draw, we must reproduce on paper exactly what we see, not what we know in our heads.

Foreshortening: The shortening of certain lines in a drawing creates a sense of space or of volume. Our eyes see objects getting smaller as they move away from us. To make objects appear three-dimensional—that is, as if they are occupying space—we must distort the actual shape of the object. This deliberate distortion can be a battle for children who are grappling with giving up their concept of how things are, to represent how they are seen.

Overlapping: Objects are superimposed to show that they are in front of or behind other objects. This creates a sense of space, although usually shallow space. Overlapping also occurs within individual objects. With all of its moving parts, the human body is a study of overlapping. I can still

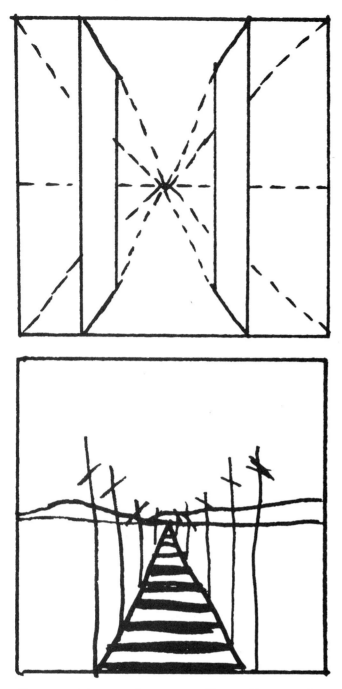

The one-point perspective system as illustrated by a set of converging lines and infamous railroad tracks

France, for example) show highly naturalistic work that represents the volume of individual animals and creates a sense of space around them. Roman paintings at Pompeii show a mastery of space through perspective. The Middle Ages showed a decided lack of interest in the representation of pictorial space. The passion for representing reality in art on the part of young people parallels that of the artists of the early Renaissance. To see how the artists of the fourteenth century "opened" the picture plane to create spatial illusions, look for reproductions of Masaccio, Masolino, Fra Angelico, Filippo Lippi, and Uccello. Uccello's work is especially appealing to young people because of his unique, almost surreal, trompe l'oeil style and his subject matter. These painters show human figures in indoor-outdoor architectural settings with plenty of complicated receding rooflines, diminishing rows of columns, foreshortened buildings, interiors, and checkered floors. Students love the costumes. Creating pictorial space was of overwhelming interest to people just emerging from the Middle Ages, an era in which symbolism was all-important and there was little interest in scientific, objective observation or realism in art. The average person was illiterate, and visual symbolism was an important means for communicating cultural and spiritual traditions. Interest in surface pattern and symbols to reflect the primary concern—other-worldly reality—superseded an interest in pictorial illusions of depth.

The focus gradually shifted from a spiritual, hierarchical system to a concern about humans and the natural world, much as a child's focus turns from parents to self as he or she begins to gain confidence in his or her ability to operate independently in the outside world. In 1435 Alberti, who invented and codified the technique of artificial perspective that dominated Italian art during the fifteenth century, wrote: "Man is the measuring rod of nature." In its substance, this exclamation is surprisingly similar to the teen or preteen's self-centered world view.

In the modern conception of perspective, diagonal lines are set up in relationship to the flat picture plane to create a sense of space. Perspective really means a viewpoint. In drawing, it is the relationship

remember the thrill when I first discovered how to show one leg in front of the other (by carefully erasing the part that was behind!).

Perspective: In the Western world, whose visual conventions we adopt as young people, various systems of perspective have been used in art through the ages. We can appreciate our children's efforts in this context. It is said that the Greeks were the first to "break through" the flat surface of the picture plane, although the much earlier cave paintings (those in Lascaux, near Montignac,

of the eye's point of view to objects in space. This relationship is represented by angles that are created by lines diagonal to the horizontal or vertical axis of the picture plane. The picture plane is flat and has right angles. Our eyes see objects appearing to recede and diminish as they move away in space. When lines of an object are drawn at a diagonal angle to the flat picture plane, the object appears to recede into the picture.

Diagonal, or orthogonal, lines can recede to converge on a single point or on multiple points on a pictorial horizon. Or, they can recede without converging. The representation of subjective reality by the use of multiple vanishing points—or objects receding in different directions—expresses the shifting relationship of our eyes to the world as we turn our heads. It is very important that the artist can deliberately move the eye and direct its attention to certain parts of a picture by using perspective.

Young people will find power in the cliché of converging railroad tracks. Here, diagonal lines converge at a single point (usually dead center, in this case) on a horizon line, thus creating a focal point of high drama. A one-point perspective system of this type can be monotonous. In a classroom, I would not offer it as a formula. (I have seen hallways full of pictures like this, all interchangeable.) To go beyond the cliché, the student must carefully observe individual instances of the relationships of angles that the lines of objects make as they exist in space. This takes time, patience, and much practice. A ruler can be held out in one's line of vision,

straight up and down on the vertical. The angles created by receding lines can be judged and reproduced on the paper. The patient observer will see that reality is more interestingly complicated than what a single formula can describe. Individual explorations of the formula can be a fascinating project and could lead to other prospects. For a class project, however, I would take the group outside to draw a street in order to sharpen the students' powers of observation. A street view, with its strong horizontal and vertical elements, demonstrates the principles of perspective clearly.

Just as color, line, pattern, and all the other elements of composition are at the mature artist's command for expressive use, so is pictorial space. It is important to note that other cultures have had much different conventions for showing space. This is an excellent topic of discussion for older students. Some Eastern art shows structures expanding as they move away in space (see screen paintings of the Edo period in Japan). Other cultures have shown objects moving up the picture plane (see medieval or early Egyptian art). Sacred art, such as Tibetan or aboriginal Australian sand painting, is not concerned with "real" space at all. As a system for the creation of the illusion of space, marking a point on a horizon line and drawing some lines receding to that point is effective, but it is not an end in itself. Many people, not just young ones, confuse illusion with art. Art is involved only when each individual artist looks deeply into himself or herself as well as outward and shows us how he or she sees.

Grandfather's Missouri Barn by Mua Merryman

Young people can begin this introspective process, but it cannot be forced any more than can the practice necessary for attaining the technical skills of representation. For the time being, the railroad ties may be interesting, but make sure to offer other inspiration, including drawings not concerned with illusions of space (nature studies by Japanese masters; people by Gauguin, Degas, and Manet; nightmares by Hieronymus Bosch; fantasy, symbol, and the inner world by Paul Klee).

Light and shade: The representation of light and shade is used to define the three-dimensionality of objects. Have students ask themselves: What am I really seeing? Avoid formulas! Shading will not cover up inaccurate drawing resulting from lack of close observation. Probably everything we need to know about drawing is to be found in Rembrandt's work. The other grand master of light and shade

was Leonardo. You might also look at Van Gogh's crosshatched drawings.

For an exercise in light and shade, make a simple still life of boxes, bottles, and fruit. Light it from one side. Then make a drawing with charcoal, filling in areas without using lines, carefully recording how light moves across the surfaces of cubes, cylinders, and spheres. Use a kneaded eraser and chamois to work light areas into dark. A kneaded eraser can be shaped like modeling clay. It can be shaped into a point, for example, to get into small, specific areas. Or, it can be stretched to clean out the charcoal dust. The chamois will take care of larger areas, is flexible, and can be shaken or washed out. You can move the charcoal around fluidly with strokes of the eraser or chamois, almost like paint.

Proportion: Proportion is the correct relation in size between two separate objects or different parts of a single object. Achieving realistic proportion can be a very tough aspect of drawing for students. The human body offers the best source of understanding the concept. Perhaps because young people still tend to "see" certain parts of an object as more important than others, heads end up too large and feet too small. And, once again, stereotypes are passed around: the cartoon formula, the awakening-to-sexual-differences formula. But what do things really look like? Only by looking and drawing exactly what they see will students understand proportion. There are ways of judging proportion, such as by holding a pencil at a certain distance from your body and noting the length of a chair or another body, as measured on the pencil, and the comparative lengths of legs, arms, backs, and so on. Perhaps the most helpful skill of all, however, is the ability to see negative space (see the discussion later in this section).

Scale: Scale concerns the relative sizes of objects. Our eyes see objects in the distance as smaller than objects in the foreground. Even young children seem quite aware of scale, whereas they may be oblivious to proportion. The influences of culture on seeing a relationship such as scale cannot be overestimated. The late Joseph Campbell, renowned scholar of mythology, told about a tribe of forest-dwelling Africans who, when brought out to view the vast space of a plain for the first time, were unable to understand the spatial reality of what they were looking at. They assumed the distant wildebeests and zebras were only the size of ants. Children's experience is similarly limited, and so is ours. We learn to see as much as is necessary for us to survive in our particular society. Imagine what we are not seeing as a result!

Butterfly by Rosalie Fanshel and *Shoe* by Mua Merryman

Negative space: Negative space can be thought of as "empty" space, space where there is no object. Learning to see it can take time. What it means is that

is as important as

The ability to see is not taught in our society, but it can be learned as surely as any skill. Seeing negative space as a positive image frees the eye from the tyranny of the idea of the object. Seeing spaces between objects helps us to place the objects in relationship to each other. Instead of looking only at an arm, look at the shape of the space between the arm and the trunk when you have your hand on your hip.

Negative space is all-important in composition. Most beginners place an object or two on the paper surrounded by empty space. But the whole surface of the picture plane is part of the picture. Concentrated time spent on learning to see negative space will facilitate effective composition.

Negative space is also the key to effective design and, as such, can be studied in advertising. For several days after the movie *Batman* swept the nation, I saw the ads for the film in the papers and had no idea what the logo was. I saw it as a mouth with rounded teeth, like the kind of false wax teeth you can get at Halloween. I was seeing the negative space as the positive image. Finally, I read the ad and saw the bat! Such is the power of negative space.

FURTHER EXPLORATIONS OF REALISTIC DRAWING

Drawing on the Right Side of the Brain, by Betty Edwards, is an excellent and enjoyable book that covers the techniques of realistic drawing well. Several of her exercises can be adapted for young people, and you may be able to create a drawing group to explore them.

For older children you might try the following:

● Provide resource books with clear, visible photographs of people, animals, buildings, and such to be used as references for what things really look like.

● Encourage the children to observe the movements of their own bodies, noting the locations of joints and the directions in which limbs can move. Tell them to work various muscles in the face. Do some dancing as a warm-up to figure drawing.

● Provide a sketch diary to document happenings with drawings. Allow rough sketches, and do not criticize. A school year is a perfect opportunity to keep a diary and practice drawing regularly.

In conclusion: Children draw naturally. It is a basic human impulse. Drawing helps them to explore the world and to integrate what they learn into their own beings with a sense of personal power about their understanding. It isn't possible to teach a young child to draw any more than it is possible to teach a baby to walk. For most young children, drawing is purely a natural activity, a form of communication, primarily internal. Parents and teachers of older children often feel out of their league with drawing because their experience with it, like that of most people, came to a halt at age eight or so. If you have older children who show a great desire to draw and an interest in learning more than you can offer, consider an instructional videotape. Be very discriminating, however, in the tape you choose. Many of these instructional tapes address only the immediate desire for simple trick techniques, and do not nurture individual creativity. As with all video viewing, an adult should be present

Above: "Monk" by Kelly McBride, age 13. Right: "The Hanging Gardens of Babylon" by Rosalie Fanshel, age 12.

to interpret. Much preferred as a how-to approach is to have the child copy a drawing or even trace one from a photograph or a quality artist's resource book. (The books from Dover Publications are excellent for this purpose.) This satisfies the desire to have something look real while allowing a student to make expressive choices.

Computer-assisted drawing is very appealing and exciting to the lucky child who has access to it. I consider computer drawings to be a form of printmaking, and I find some of the results exciting indeed. Although many professionals are working in this new medium solely to produce works that are an end in themselves, this way of making prints (along with the creative use of copy machines), though intriguing, has more application to graphic arts than fine art. What is missing from the electronic medium is the delicate energy of the human hand powered by thirty-five different muscles exquisitely conveying thoughts and emotions directly from their source.

PAINTING

TIME Allow at least 30 minutes per painting session.

MATERIALS Liquid tempera paint: Red, yellow, blue, green, orange, violet, black, and white are essential. Magenta, turquoise, and burnt sienna are also useful. Brands vary a lot; I use Kaylor for good-quality, bright colors in 16-ounce squeeze bottles.

Brushes: Soft, flat bristle brushes in $\frac{1}{4}$-, $\frac{1}{2}$-, and 1-inch widths. Buy as many brushes as you can (one for each color is recommended). Buy a few wider brushes and a set of assorted small brushes (pointed, flat, and so on) for details. Cut-up sponges can also be used for large areas.

Paper: Buy 18- by 24-inch newsprint, or explore sources of free paper from printers and designers. I provide smaller paper also, but the large sizes are essential.

Paint containers: Styrofoam egg cartons and meat trays for palettes; heavy, wide-mouthed jars

DOING IT As the facilitator, you must have some basic knowledge about color. This is not information to be forced on the children, but rather to inform your comments about their work and to bring certain possibilities to their attention. The following are some basic concepts.

The primary colors are RED, YELLOW, and BLUE. They are pure—they can't be made from mixing any other colors. Theoretically, they can be mixed in individual combinations to make all the other colors. However, even good-quality paint doesn't always mix according to color theory; cheap paint with lots of filler is unreliable and rarely mixes well. Adding the primaries together yields the following new colors:

RED + YELLOW = ORANGE
RED + BLUE = VIOLET
BLUE + YELLOW = GREEN

The secondary colors are ORANGE, VIOLET, and GREEN. When mixed with the primaries, the secondary colors yield:

RED + ORANGE = RED-ORANGE
YELLOW + ORANGE = YELLOW-ORANGE
RED + VIOLET = RED-VIOLET
BLUE + VIOLET = BLUE-VIOLET
YELLOW + GREEN = YELLOW-GREEN
BLUE + GREEN = BLUE-GREEN

Mixing primaries and secondaries results in tertiary colors. You can continue to mix colors ad infinitum for varying hues of violet, for example: red-violet-red, blue-violet-blue, etc.

Complementary colors are certain pairs of hues. Each pair is composed of one primary and one secondary. Red and green, yellow and violet, and blue and orange are complementary pairs. In each pair, the secondary color contains the two primaries that are not its complementary primary. Complementary pairs are equal but opposite on the color wheel, a device showing hue relationships.

Complements are equal in their demands on our visual attention. Johannes Itten describes this effect in *The Elements of Color*: "[Complements] are opposite, they require each other. They incite each other to maximum vividness when adjacent. . . . The remarkable physiological fact, as yet unexplained, [is] that the eye requires any given color to be balanced by the complementary. . . ." Therefore, using complements side by side produces a special effect. Our eye muscles actually work to keep the colors separate, resulting in an illusion of vibration, especially when the complements are also of equal value as with red and green.

Value refers to the qualities of lightness and darkness across which a particular color can range. White and black affect value. They aren't hues themselves (in color theory, black is the absence of all light and white is the mixture of all hues); rather, they lighten and darken hues, resulting in tints and shades.

Hues relate differently when their values are changed. A light blue and a dark orange placed next to each other, while still complements, do not relate as intensely as when they are of equal value. Shades may also be produced by adding a small amount of a color's complement to its mate. The resulting shade has a different quality than a shade made with black. Generally, adding a complement yields a richer effect because you are shading with hue as well as with value. When complements are mixed in equal amounts, they make gray or black.

Intensity refers to the degree of saturation, or how much pigment is contained in a particular hue. Compared to high-quality paint, cheap paint has less saturation of pigment and uses more filler; therefore, it often looks dead after it dries, and it doesn't mix well.

Warmth and *coolness* are properties of color with great expressive potential. As with all color, effects are relative. But, in general, hot or warm colors are

Above left and below: Proud painters display their work . . . the universal language of children.

Above: Generous supplies and elbowroom pay off in ability of children to concentrate and excel in their creativity.
Opposite: Paintings by Joseph Sanchez

those associated with the sun, earth, fire, and opacity. Cool colors are those associated with shadow, air, water, and transparency. The works of the Impressionists are especially effective for demonstrating the concepts of warm and cool colors to children. The paintings of Renior and Monet can make you perspire and grab for sunglasses or shiver and reach for a sweater.

An understanding of hue, value, and intensity is essential to making an informed assessment of a painting. Experimentation is, of course, the best way to understand these concepts.

The list that follows presents some exercises that you can do and even suggest to children.

1. Mix all the colors you can on a large sheet of paper. Use brushes to mix the paints directly on the paper one by one, in a systematic manner, or follow your whim if you choose.

2. Make as many shades and tints of a green (or red, or brown or whatever) as you can, mixing on the paper with different amounts of black and white.

3. Make as many shades of gray as you can ranging from white to black.

4. Make a simple still life by using one dominant hue and as many variations of it as you can. Add touches of its complement here and there—don't try to represent the real color of the objects you are painting; instead, make an arbitrary decision to make a "blue picture." Be Picasso in his blue period. Do a similar painting but reverse the situation, making the complement dominate.

For exploration in the classroom, easels are wonderful, but they can be frustrating for children working with paint that runs. Use both easels and tabletops, if possible. Painting should always be done standing up, except for very small work that can be reached and seen in its entirety from a sitting

position. (You will notice that small children sitting down will paint only the bottom third of the paper.)

Have a brush available for each color so there's no need to wash brushes frequently (which will result in watered-down colors.) Styrofoam egg cartons make excellent containers for small amounts of several colors. Leave empty spaces in the carton for mixing new colors. Short, heavy, wide-mouthed jars are great for holding paint in the trays of easels.

Colors can be used straight from the tube or mixed. Encourage the children not to be satisfied with the limited number of hues available from the paint jars. Demonstrate how to mix colors in egg cartons, on Styrofoam trays, or right on the paper. Make children aware that the green of a pine tree is not the green of a lime; that tree trunks are not solid brown, but may contain green, yellow, red, orange, violet, and gray; that city streets are pink, under certain circumstances; that skin has blue and red veins underneath that color the lighter shades of skin. Because children are taught to know that an apple is red and the sky is blue, they may never learn to see exactly what colors exist unless you show them. Teach them to rely on their own sight.

Some basic concepts that might not necessarily be obvious to children are these:

1. Don't add water to tempera paint.

2. Use a small brush for a small job and a large brush for a large job.

3. Don't torture brushes. Small sponges may be used to cover large areas.

4. Hold brushes loosely, as if shaking hands. You can brace your arm against your body to steady your hand. Don't hold a brush as you would hold a pencil.

5. Use a Styrofoam meat tray or plastic plate as a palette for mixing special colors. You can hold it in your hand while painting.

6. To lighten tempera colors, you need much more white in proportion to color. To avoid waste, always add dabs of color to white, a bit at a time, rather than white to color.

Many children's first paintings consist of colored lines set on paper. They are really an extension of drawing until the child realizes the full potential of paint. Painting whole areas should be encouraged but not turned into an assignment. You can talk about covering the whole paper with paint and show the children reproductions to see how the "empty space" is actually full of color. Just seeing some exciting paintings can be enough encouragement. Go to the library and check out books about Egyptian paintings, Indian miniatures, Fra Angelico, Van Gogh, Paul Klee, Grandma Moses, Wayne Thiebaud, David Hockney, Joan Brown, or Oliver Jackson. Do some reading and looking, and then share

Above: Working on a flat surface prevents unwanted drips; standing allows small children to see their work. Opposite: Extend the possibilities of paint by adding other media like stamps and crayons. Rosemarie Perez has used even the end of her paintbrush to etch lines in the paint.

with the children what you discover. There's no need for them to be little art historians who can drop names and memorize styles. The goal is to elicit from each child his or her own style.

Almost all children want to paint; some are driven to paint. Most children with little art experience will hang onto stereotypes such as a rainbows, flowers, and rockets. Some will never seem to get be-

Painting **29**

Walt Castro, age 11, uses a Stryofoam tray to plan out his colors before applying them.

yond these, but who's to say when this repetition will lead to original work? If a child prefers to mimic commercial imagery, do not be critical but do not give enthusiastic praise. Instead, emphasize how interested you are in what a person can tell you in paint about himself or herself. Sometimes "Show me your house" or "Describe your family" will start a new theme going. When making suggestions, don't underestimate your influence. Because children are so eager to do what adults do, we have a great responsibility to make sure that, in trying to guide, we don't prescribe.

Content can be discussed by looking at the paintings of the masters. Point out that some of them paint from their imagination and some paint what is directly in front of them. I enjoy showing children the paintings of Henri Rousseau, a self-taught artist who worked from his imagination, photos, and paintings. Although he never went to the African or Latin American jungles, he painted monkeys and leopards in lush scenes that children love to get lost in. Children also enjoy Paul Klee and Marc Chagall.

For younger children, painting is not an imitation of reality but a reality of its own, where people are doing things and making other things happen. It is pure visual storytelling. Imitation of reality isn't important. Older children trying to capture the look of

a tree or an animal need some guidance and should be referred to the real thing—or at least to photographs. Even though these children can be adamant about making their work look real, they don't look closely to see how something is actually shaped, any more than they look to see what color something actually is. The society in which we live influences how we see. This is demonstrated dramatically by individuals from "primitive" societies who are not able to see themselves in photographs or judge distances or maintain a sense of perspective when their environment is changed. In our society, we do not learn to really see what we look at. We register superficial data and move on. Even very talented children must practice the skill of really seeing.

Some people are by nature visual. Some who are not so much so still love to paint because of the expressive, sensual pleasure of painting. Photography has shown that the function of art is not simply the imitation of reality. Order is being made, knowledge is being integrated, feelings are being expressed, power is being wielded. To quote Frank Sieberling: "Art . . . supplies an area—a kind of testing ground—for the expression of viewpoints or insights without penalty. This frees it to experiment and to illumine, often to lead the way."

PAPER PROJECTS

COLLAGES

TIME At least 30 minutes at a time

MATERIALS White glue (Elmer's School Glue); mix with water, about 1 part water to 3 parts glue

Scissors

Medium- to heavy-stock paper or board for background (be sure to explore local printers and shops as sources for free paper)

Collage materials: Colored paper scraps; colored tissue; wallpaper pieces; wrapping paper or other interesting papers; high-quality magazines (such as *National Geographic*, *Sports Illustrated*, *Smithsonian*, *Scientific American*); photographs (you can photocopy them and enlarge or reduce them); and an assortment of miscellany, such as seed catalogs, ticket stubs, flyers, stickers, fabric scraps, yarn, computer art, and rubber-stamp prints

Tempera paint, oil pastels, colored pencils and pens, crayons

Optional equipment: copy machine

Provide as many opportunities for collage as possible. Adult supervision is not necessary.

DOING IT Collage provides a wonderful opportunity not only to communicate ideas but to participate directly in the manipulation of the formal elements of picture making. Whole chunks of space can be filled quickly, and these chunks are the building blocks of pictures. The ability to manipulate images quickly and to juxtapose the unlikely or the ironic provides a great sense of power. Young people can spend hours on collage. They become

totally involved in the process and rarely want to leave anything unfinished.

Collage is a contemporary art form that developed with the advent of easily available, inexpensive paper, mass media, photography, and photocopies. The earliest examples you can find at the library will probably be from the Cubist era (1906 through 1925); from this period, look for the collages of Picasso and Braque. In contemporary times, there are many more collage artists, such as Romare Bearden, who portrayed his Southern, African-American origins and reflected an art heavily influenced by jazz. Some artists, such as Robert Rauschenberg, have taken collage a step further and attach actual objects to their canvases.

Before you begin, set out the materials along with a good selection of magazines and other papers. Collage lends itself to working on a large scale, so

Fabric sample collage by Rosalie Fanshel (below left) and detail of mixed-media collage by the author (above)

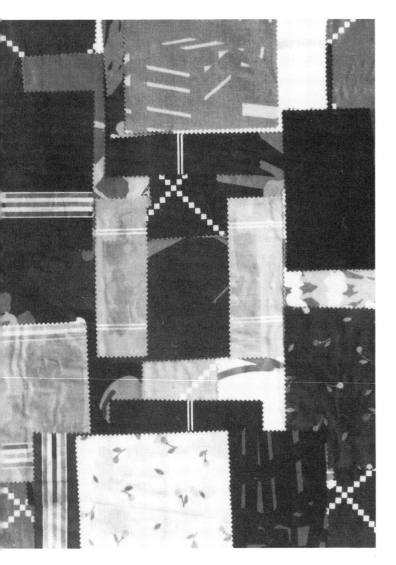

there should be lots of elbowroom. For a work space, four individual desks can be pushed together and another used to hold papers. A large work table can hold a can full of scissors; an egg carton of tempera paints; three or four containers of glue (thinned with water for easy brushing); and a box or two of other drawing materials, such as crayons or oil pastels. Keep extra boxes of magazines and other materials under the table. Then simply cut or tear and glue. Brush on the glue. Paint, oil pastels, and such can be worked into the surface to unify a picture.

Magazines of all kinds (nature, fashion, or sports) are intriguing to all ages. Wrapping papers are another wonderful source of material. Collect foils and glazed papers from Christmas, weddings, Valentine's Day, and so on.

Making a tissue collage is an excellent way to learn about color, since the paper is translucent and colors will "mix." This process achieves a beautiful stained-glass look. Use thinned glue (in this case, 1 part water to 1 part glue). Paint glue on the background paper, lay down the tissue, then brush the top of the tissue with glue.

Fabric collages require a heavy-stock background. Upholstery or decorator shops may have fabric sample selections to give away. These selections can be interesting because they contain one fabric or design in several colors or textures. For a fabric project, use a stronger solution of glue.

WEAVINGS

TIME One or more 30-minute period

MATERIALS Construction paper or other heavy paper, any shape

Scissors

This project is for ages six and older. All members of a large group can work at once.

DOING IT Have the children fold the paper in half and cut parallel slits to within about 1 inch from the edge of the paper, which makes a paper frame that holds the parallel strips (the "warp") in place. Then cut strips of paper (the "weft") in a variety of colors to be woven in and out of the warp strips in the paper frame.

Cutting their own papers is interesting to children, and it gives them a chance to gain control of small motor muscles. There is no point to this project if everything is precut. The finished weaving should not be presented as a holiday table-mat project. Instead, realize that you are giving students the opportunity to work with the checkerboard pattern, which is a very basic pattern (along with the stripe and diamond), and to weave wonderful combinations of light and dark by using different colors and sizes of strips. Tack the finished products to the wall so they may be appreciated as art.

Paper weaving by Chandra Vozobule

MOLAS

TIME One or more 30-minute periods

MATERIALS Construction paper, 12 by 18 inches

Scissors

Pencils

White glue or paste

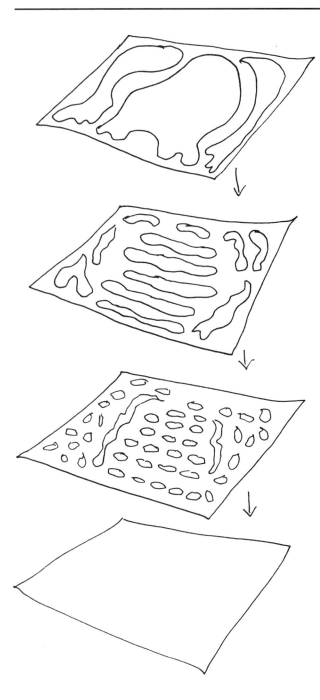

This project is a brainstorm of workshop teacher Nora Fanshel. It is based on the layered fabric panels of the Cuna Indians (who originally incorporated the panels into clothing) from the San Blas Islands in Panama's Gulf of Darien. Before suggesting this project to children, make a paper mola for yourself, to see how the process works. It's easy to find books about the molas of the Cuna Indians to use as examples.

DOING IT Use from two to seven full sheets of construction paper for each mola. Draw a large design on what will be the top layer and cut it out. The design can be one large central shape or two or three shapes with lots of room for successive layers to show through from underneath. The first (top) layer should contain the larger elements; the elements in the following layers should be within the boundaries established by the first layer. Draw more elements of the design and cut through each successive layer to reveal several colors of paper. Alternatively, the paper can be carefully torn instead of cut—tearing produces interesting edges. Apply paste or glue between layers starting with the bottom two layers, and working up to the top.

RUBBINGS

TIME At least 30 minutes at a time

MATERIALS Newsprint paper

Thick crayons

Optional: Thin cardboard, sturdy

cardboard, scissors, glue, and brushes for glue (for making patterns for rubbing)

DOING IT My wonderful co-teacher, Nora Fanshel, has the students go on a "treasure hunt" for objects to rub. They can start with the bottom of their own shoes and move on to ventilation grates, ornamental hardware, woodwork, or tree leaves. It is best to use wide, soft crayons with a big piece of lightweight paper like newsprint. Place the paper over the object to be rubbed and use the flat side of the crayon to make the rubbing. The rubbings can be cut out and used in a collage.

You can make your own patterns to rub by cutting and gluing thin pieces of cardboard onto a sturdy cardboard backing. The patterns or pictures can be simple or complex and, using crayons of different colors, you can make multiple rubbings from the same pattern.

You may take a field trip to an old graveyard with interesting headstones, or to other sites in your community to make rubbings. In Asia, rice paper is used to make rubbings of ancient temple carvings.

This rubbing was made using crayon over newsprint and everyday objects, including the sole of the artist's shoe (center).

DRINKING-STRAW CONSTRUCTIONS

TIME At least 30 minutes to start; after that the project can be worked on indefinitely.

MATERIALS Sturdy drinking straws (not the flexible kind)

String

Wire (medium-strength wire that bends but holds its shape) to use

as needles for threading string through straws

Scissors

Pliers

This is a project I learned about from sculptor Ruth Asawa at an art education conference. She learned it from Buckminster Fuller (creator of the geodesic dome), who designed the activity for young people. Buckminster Fuller invented a new world map, the dymaxion sky-ocean world map, which is based on the same principle as that of the straw sculptures. The map is made out of triangles that fold together into a sphere but, when unfolded,

show the relationship of continents more accurately, as a one-world island in a one-world ocean. To learn more, look at his book, *Critical Path*. The map is an example of how one person, working with the simple idea of the triangle, came up with a whole new world view. This project is not appropriate for children under nine. If done with a large group, extra adult help will be needed to get constructions started.

DOING IT With the pliers, make a small loop, or eye, at the end of the wire. Attach a length of string, as long as can be easily handled while being threaded through straws. Thread the string through three straws and form a triangle. Tie the string securely to hold the triangle together. This is the basic unit.

Building on the triangle base, you can make a three-dimensional pyramid; add these straws by tying a new length of string to a corner, threading it through the straw, and pushing the straw in place at the joint. Add two more straws at the other corners, and join them together at the top of the structure (making the point of the pyramid).

How many of these structures do you need to make a base of a much larger pyramid? Let the children answer by doing it. They will figure out the answer as they go along. The pyramid can be the beginning of larger, more complicated structures as more sides are added in all directions. For instance, try making a sphere with triangles as the basic unit. Perhaps your school playground has a dome-shaped climbing structure the students can examine.

This project is especially fascinating for the three-dimensionally minded, and these constructions make lovely art objects when hung from the ceiling and allowed to rotate in air currents.

LANTERNS

TIME One or two 20-minute sessions

MATERIALS Colored tissue paper

Sturdy balloons

White glue (diluted to 1 part glue

to 1 part water)

Brushes for glue

Sequins or glitter

Scissors

Yarn (for hanging the lantern)

Needle (for yarn)

DOING IT Blow up a balloon and tie it tightly. The tissue is applied in the same way as for tissue collage (page 32). Cover the entire balloon with at least four layers of tissue. When the paper is dry, pop the balloon. It will deflate, sucking in the sides of the lantern (scaring everybody), but once you have carefully removed the balloon, you can reach your hand in and straighten out the sides. Neatly trim the opening. Shiny glitter or other such decoration can also be applied. (I generally avoid glitter, but it does have appeal for certain projects.) To provide a means of hanging the lantern, sew a piece of yarn through the top of the lantern.

Renée Schomp's lantern becomes magic with a heavy coating of glitter.

ORIGAMI BOXES

TIME About 15 minutes to make the first box

MATERIALS Construction paper, wallpaper, or   Rulers

origami paper   Scissors

Pencils

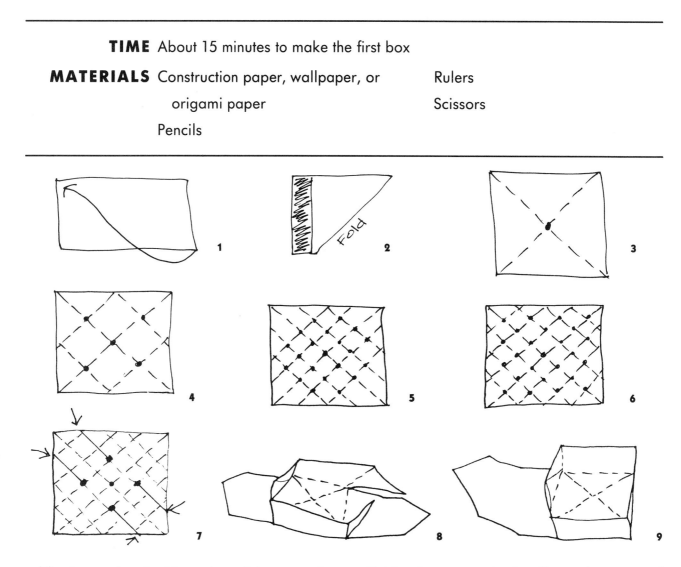

The instructions in this section tell how to make a simple box form. To make other shapes, consult one of the many wonderful books available that children can follow on their own. A box form can be made into steadily increasing or decreasing sizes so that you end up with a nest of boxes. This activity serves as a super applied math project when done with rulers and carefully monitored measurements. Or just try it without measuring, which may be tedious for some.

DOING IT You will need a square piece of paper. Fold a rectangle diagonally, as shown. Trim excess. Unfold and fold opposite corners, crease and unfold; repeat so that you have an *X*. Put a pencil dot on the intersection of the *X*.

Fold each corner to the dot. Crease the paper and open it. Mark the new intersections with dots. Then fold each corner to the intersection farthest away from it. Crease the paper and open it.

Now fold each corner to the closest intersection; crease and open the paper. The grid is now completed. Make four cuts, as indicated.

To form the box, fold the corner of the larger cut sections to the first intersection; fold the sections over once more. Make this side of the box stand up, and fold forward one third from each pointed end of the box at right angles with the middle third. Do this to the opposite section. The sides will overlap each other. Then fold the two remaining long sides up and over the sides just formed. Crease them into place.

HOT WAX PAINTINGS

TIME From 5 to 30 minutes. Adult supervision will be needed with electrical appliances.

MATERIALS Crayons pieces (old broken ones are fine)

Drawing paper, construction paper, or card stock

Old paint brushes

Electric hot tray

Aluminum foil or an old muffin tin

Bottle corks or pencils with erasers

Wax, or encaustic, painting goes back at least as far as the Greeks. Many of those lovely white marble statues were originally brightly colored.

DOING IT There are two ways to paint with hot wax. For the first, cover the hot tray with aluminum foil. When it's warmed up, put a piece of paper on the tray. While you work, hold the paper in place with a cork or the eraser end of a pencil. Hold the pieces of crayon on the warmed paper until they start to melt, then move them around and "paint" with the melting wax. For older children, melt the crayon bits in an old muffin tin on the hot tray and paint directly with this waxy color.

WAX RESISTS

Make a crayon drawing on paper. Then choose a color of tempera paint and mix it with water to achieve a watercolor-like consistency. Brush the tempera across the painting. It will color the areas not touched by the crayon and bead up on the waxy areas, creating an atmospheric curtain of color.

Above and below left: Hot wax painting details show fluidity and texture that is so appealing to young artists. Metallic crayons make especially exciting results.

CRAYON ETCHINGS

This technique is great for detail-oriented people. Cover a piece of drawing paper or cardboard with patches of crayon color. With another color, preferably a dark one, work over the entire surface, covering all the patches of color. Then "etch" through the dark layer with a toothpick or other sharp object (we used bobby pins, in my childhood). Paul Klee's painting *Fish Magic* was done in oils but its effect of glowing color emerging from a dark setting resembles the result that this way of working produces.

CLAY

I started with some clay and made a pinched cup. I turned it into a triceratops. I pinched out a head and tail and then I pinched out some horns, then I made a line with my fingers around the bottom. I made a line and then I pushed up the clay around the legs up to the line. That made the legs. Then I made a hole that didn't go all the way through on its back. Then I made a little caveman sitting down to go in the hole. I made it so it could come out. And out of the scraps, I made another little triceratops—like a baby of the other one. Then I made another little hole in the back of the baby one, and then I made a little caveman sitting down for that one. And that was the baby of the other caveman. I only had a little pinch left. I didn't use that.

—David, age eight and a half

Reputable ceramics companies can inform you as to which clays and glazes are approved for use with elementary children in your state. Don't be intimidated by the thought of working with clay if you have no experience with the medium. Though it's best to work with an experienced instructor, you can learn a lot on your own from making basic hand-built items such as the ones in this chapter. And don't give up on clay because you don't have a kiln. You can take the clay objects that you and the children make to a ceramics shop. For a certain price per load, you can have a professional fire the work for you. Find out in advance how much work makes a load (you will probably want to save up work or go in with someone else). The following materials list looks long, but you already have some supplies and the rest are not expensive. See "Wedging," later in this chapter, for how to make a wedging table. Materials for glazing are listed in the section titled "Glazing Your Ceramics" (page 53).

TIME Two 30- to 40-minute sessions on consecutive days to work with clay, approximately one week for clay to dry, and two days for firing and cooling before the clay is ready to glaze. Glazing time is discussed under "Glazing Your Ceramics," later in this chapter.

MATERIALS Clay: Clay comes in 25-pound sacks. About 6 pounds of clay per child is enough for each student to make two or three finished pieces. Clay is sticky earth. There are several kinds of ceramic clay. If you are making pieces to fire, find out at what temperature the kiln operator will fire your load. Discuss the project and the firing conditions with your ceramics dealer before experimenting. Before you buy, look at and feel samples of fired clay. Depending on the composition of the

MATERIALS clay, fired surfaces vary; some are of better quality than others. Look for a close-grained clay that is not too rough or porous (this makes it hard for children to glaze). Too much talc (a powdery additive) can make clay weak and rough. Look for material with enough grog (crushed, fired clay that adds texture and reduces shrinkage) to make the clay workable for children.

Clay-working tools: A few professional clay-working tools will be useful. Wooden tools for shaping clay and metal trimming tools with loops of various sizes and shapes are available. Children appreciate real tools, although most are content with their hands. You will also need forks and knives (the garage-sale variety), rolling pins, and nails of various sizes.

Cutting "wire": Fishing line is great for slicing clay. Cut a 24-inch-long piece of line and tie each end securely around a Popsicle stick (or some other sturdy stick). You will hold a stick in each hand as you pull the fishing line through the clay, toward you, to cut off a slice.

Cloth: Clay sticks to wood or Formica-type surfaces. So, if the tabletops in your classroom are made of these materials, you will need pieces of canvas or burlap, about 20 inches wide by 26 long, on which to work with the clay. Plaster surfaces are ideal for working with clay and can be made by pouring plaster into forms. (See "Wedging," later in this chapter, to learn how to make a plaster table for wedging.) However, canvas or burlap works well—clay lifts off either one easily. Provide a place mat–sized piece of cloth for each child, to define work areas, and provide a larger cloth for children to use when rolling out slabs (taking turns).

Wood slats: Buy or prepare wood slats that are ½ inch by about 15 inches. Use scraps of baseboard molding or lath. Provide two slats per rolling pin.

Objects to create texture: Gather whatever you can think of that would be interesting to press into clay—seashells, ice trays, doorknobs, stones, kitchen tools (a meat tenderizer is one of my favorites), pinecones, bicycle handles, lace, and so on.

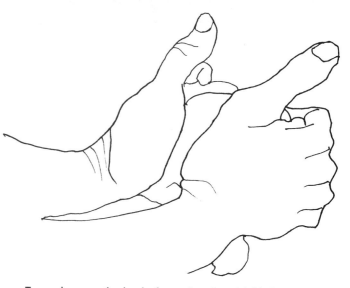

To wedge, use the heel of your hand and fold clay over and over to remove all air pockets.

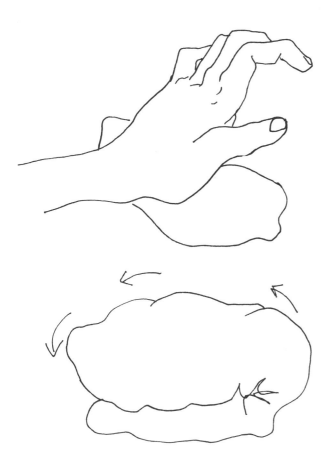

WEDGING

Brand-new sacks of clay, from a supplier with a good turnover, are ready to use and don't need to be wedged, or banged and kneaded. However, if clay has been stored for several months, the clay molecules tend to line up in the same direction. This can result in fractures along these lines when the clay is fired. Drop the sacks of clay on a cement floor a few times to shake up molecules if you suspect the clay has been sitting for a while. Clay that has been previously used must be wedged to eliminate air pockets. Otherwise, when heated during kiln firing, the air pockets will expand, and may even break the piece or cause it to explode. If you are working with young children, you will need to wedge the clay. They can watch and practice by wedging their leftover scraps at the end of a session. A whole session on learning to wedge might be set aside for older children.

Making a surface for wedging: The ideal space for working with clay includes a wedging table, a table with plaster of paris surface. If you plan to use clay on a regular basis, you may want to make a wedging table. The job involves pouring plaster

into a permanent form made of two-by-fours nailed together to build a frame approximately 28 inches wide by 20 inches long by 3 inches thick, or to the dimensions necessary to fit an existing counter or table. Nail a piece of sturdy 1-inch-thick plywood to this frame of two-by-fours into which the plaster will be poured. Cut a piece of chicken wire that fits inside the form; you will insert it later. Place the form on level ground covered with newspaper for protection if necessary. To fill a 28- by 20-inch form, you will need one 100-pound sack of plaster of paris or five 20-pound sacks. To mix the plaster, use a clean wheelbarrow or large, heavy-duty plastic bucket. Fill the container two-thirds full of water. Using a large coffee can or small bucket, gently sift can-fulls of plaster over water, letting it sink without stirring until the plaster has reached a level just under the level of the water's surface. Now stir gently with a smooth, flat stick to prevent introducing air bubbles. Pour the plaster directly from the wheelbarrow or bucket into the frame, filling it halfway. Then stop and place the chicken wire into the form and continue adding the wet plaster until the form is full. Smooth off the top of the plaster with a strip of cardboard or wood.

After the plaster is dry to the touch (depending on weather, this may take a few days), you will need a helper to lift it to its permanent place in the workspace.

You don't need a fancy table to wedge clay, however. Just lay canvas over a tabletop and anchor it in place by pinning it or lacing it underneath, ironing

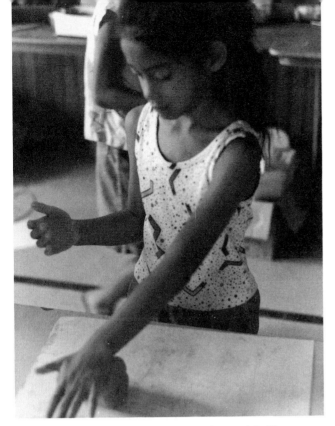

Wedging (above) and rolling slabs (below right): Clay responds directly to children's touch and provides a physical balance to time spent in more cerebral pursuits, such as studying concepts, and to passive activities, such as TV viewing.

board–style. Make sure the canvas is secure; you don't want it to slip.

Wedging the clay: To wedge a lump of clay, bang it down to flatten it. Working with both hands, fold the far edge toward you with your fingers while pressing with the heels of your hands. Continue folding and pressing. You will develop a rhythm, pulling the edge forward with your fingers and pressing with the heels of your hands. When the clay seems to be shaping into a solid mass, cut through it with your "wire" to look for air holes. Keep wedging until they are gone, then slap the pieces together, wedge a few more times, and you're ready.

DOING IT I strongly recommend that children be given time to work with clay without having to make anything, especially if working in a public-school classroom where clay is not frequently used. On the first day, have all the tools available, including the variety of objects for pressing. Stand back while the children do all the pounding and slapping and squishing they want. Some will try to make something and ask for help; others will need

another day or more just to pound and squish. In a classroom, where activities are geared to a large group, this first day of exploration is crucial: The children have time to get acquainted with the clay before committing themselves to a goal. Before distributing the clay, make sure the students understand that, at the end of the half hour, they will put the clay in a bag and wait until the next day to begin pieces they will keep. Doing it the following day is important; their appetite for the work is whetted.

If the used clay is too wet, spread it on a canvas-covered or a plaster tabletop (which will absorb exesss moisture) for a few hours. When sticky sogginess is gone, wedge it well. If the clay is still too sticky, layer it with dryish clay and put it in a bag for a couple of days.

If the clay is too dry, slice it into 1-inch slabs, poke holes in them with your thumb, and sprinkle water into the holes. Stack slices and place them in a bag (you can also alternate wet and dry slices, as previously described). When the moisture seems to have returned, wedge the clay well. You may need to repeat the moistening process until you get the consistency of fresh clay. If the material is just a bit stiff but not terribly dry, I sometimes add a few drops of water to the bag and the clay seems to absorb it after a few days. Allow several weeks to prepare too-wet or too-dry clay for use.

PINCHED FORMS

DOING IT

Using wire, slice off a 3- to 4-inch piece of clay. Give children a big lump of clay at first. Starting out with a stingy amount produces stingy work. If they begin having trouble, remove some clay.

BASIC PINCH POT

Begin by demonstrating how to shape a lump of clay into a ball. Bang it on a table, knocking down corners to round it out and then shaping it into a rough round glob about the size of a tennis ball. They can work with you. There should be lots of satisfying banging and slapping of clay. With the clay ball on the table, press a thumb into the center. Turn the ball and press your thumb against your fingers. Now put both thumbs in and continue to turn and pinch the clay outward and upward. Nudging with the fingers and pressing up with the thumbs will create a tall pot. Nudging and pressing out will create a wide, flatish pot. Pay attention to the thickness of the walls. I tell the students to "listen to your fingers" and try to press evenly around the pot so it isn't pinched too thin in one spot and left too thick in another. The key to pinching is the pressure of fingers against each other, with the clay in the middle being gently shaped, expanded, moved. Quiet concentration is important. It's a good idea to make some practice pots on your own, then slice them through with a wire to check the thickness of the walls. Demonstrate this for the children. Depending on the type of clay, ask your clay dealer about the optimal wall thickness for the clay you are using. Don't worry too much if the children have trouble making walls of uniform thickness; it's more important that they not be too thick or too thin.

Some children will inadvertently press down too hard and create a pot bottom so thin that it stays behind on the table when you pick up the pot. If the whole bottom is gone, start over. Small holes in the sides or a too-thin bottom can be easily repaired by applying bits of clay with your thumb and smoothing them into the pot. Though I'm against working on a student's project, if a child has just put considerable effort into a pot, I will certainly help repair it, having the student do the final touches. Another common problem results when students pinch out the side walls only and end up with very thick pot bottoms. Use a clay tool with a loop to remove the excess clay, without changing the shape of the pot.

Pinch pots can be finished any way you like: You can leave them as they are, or you can smooth them, press textured items into their sides (shells, wire mesh, a hair brush, or the like), or decorate them with designs drawn with a dull pencil or clay tool. This is a matter of taste. You can broaden children's impulses by offering several possibilities, but you'll find they have their own ideas that are certain to emerge and develop. Parents may not always understand what children are capable of when allowed to work on their own like this. It is a gift to the child to accept him or her as is. Once I greatly admired a first-effort pinch pot by a kindergartner for the liveliness of the imprints left by little fingers working. Later I found out that her mother was unhappy that "no one had taught her how to smooth it out."

It is important to understand that the interior space of a pinch pot is not a hole, but a positive space that determines the outside shape. Young children may not grasp this concept verbally, but they understand it intuitively, and using correct terminology will solidify their understanding.

OTHER PINCHED FORMS

A very basic characteristic of clay is that it shrinks when it dries. Pieces that stick when wet will almost always fall off when dry. This is especially true of the little balls of clay and other shapes that most young people stick on for details. These should definitely be pinched out instead. I have begun to stress creating animal and other forms by pinching because it results in strong pieces with appendages that don't fall off when the clay is dry.

It takes some effort to help a child see how pinch-

ing works, but it is worth the time. It is difficult for children to see how a horse shape, for example, is going to come out of a ball of clay; sticking things on comes much more naturally. The stick-on technique is an additive approach closely resembling drawing, which is familiar to most children. All pieces that are not pinched out must be scored before joining. Use a kitchen fork to incise deep crisscrossing grooves on both joining surfaces. Most children will run the fork too lightly across the clay, so check their work the first time they are joining pieces.

Candleholders and cups (above) wait to be fired. Glazed finished product (below) by Rosalie, age 13, looks good enough to eat. All closed forms are hollow.

Human shapes: Start with a ball of clay. Roll it so it elongates, and then pinch out a head shape. Pinch into the upper sides to bring out arms; do the same with the lower half to create legs. If it is going to be a standing figure, put it upright now and press the legs of the figure against the table to form feet. When the figure is steady, the details can be worked out. You'll find most children want to get at those details right away, before erecting the figure, and it is necessary to explain to them that their efforts will be erased when they press the piece to make it stand up. As is often true with art, the characteristics of the medium will teach the artist discipline, even if the artist is initially unwilling.

Animal shapes: It's very helpful to have a picture of the animal to work from, so the students can

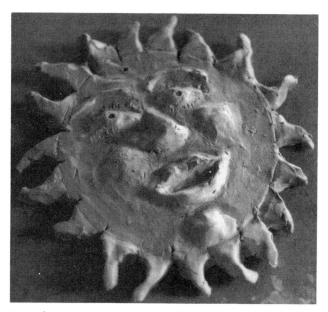

A sun by Mua Merryman, age 10, started as a slab; thicker parts are hollowed from behind.

see how far below the head and neck the legs are, where they connect, and so on. The children can form the head, body, fore-, and hind legs just as they would for a human figure. Animal figures will, of course, generally be positioned horizontally rather than vertically. A tail can be pinched out, the form modified and shaped, the neck defined, the back curved, and the legs positioned so they support the body. Pinched-out legs are far superior to added-on legs. Over and over again, I have seen children try to add skinny "snakes" of clay under a

heavy body. They are rarely strong enough to support the body, not to mention the difficulty of getting them all the same length. Pinched-out legs can be evened out by pressing the animal on the table gently. Then the details can be added. Beware of long, skinny tails. They will almost certainly break. Instead, show how a tail can be curved to lie against the body. Ancient clay animals frequently display this technique.

I always demonstrate the pinched-animal method because of the difficulty of envisioning the head and limbs coming out of a ball of clay. But children should use their own piece of clay for their creation. The demo piece can be left for reference.

Very young children will be satisfied once the basic parts are roughly defined. Older ones can make finely detailed forms from these clumpy beginnings. Every once in a while, I encounter children who just cannot get this way of working. When I see such children in trouble, I let them work the way they need to, even if parts fall off later. It is important to strike a balance between letting the children explore on their own and giving them the helpful instruction that will make their piece work.

Animal pots: Children often come up with this ancient idea on their own. While making the basic pinch pot, heads, tails, wings, and other appendages can be pinched out. The limit of imagination is the only limit here. Once, a boy made a duck pot in a classroom where I was helping. Later, I found a picture of a prehistoric pot that was almost identical. Check out some library books on ancient Chinese, pre-Columbian (Mexican), African, Indian, or early Greek pottery. Show the children. Working with clay is as old as humanity. By looking at the similarities between works made thousands of years ago and their own pieces, children develop a sense of history, and of being connected to humanity as a whole in a world that can often seem chaotic.

Combined pinch pots: Two pinch pots can be put together to make a hollow ball shape. Be certain to make a tiny air hole with a nail so hot air can escape during firing. Also, use a fork to score the surfaces that are to join, so they will grip and stay together when dry.

Lids and handles for pinch pots: Lid shapes

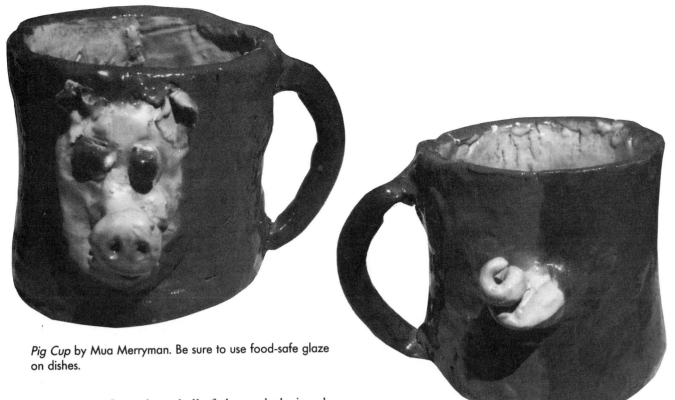

Pig Cup by Mua Merryman. Be sure to use food-safe glaze on dishes.

are made by flattening a ball of clay and placing the pots on them upside down. Cut away any clay beyond the edge of the pot, so the lid will fit. A little snake of clay or three little balls can be added as stops (pinched out or scored on) to fit inside the pot so the lid doesn't slide around. Lids should dry on top of pots so the shapes conform. If a lid is sagging, put a ball of newspaper inside the pot in order to support the lid.

If handles are desired, score clay if possible. Push the clay together at the joining place, taking care not to pinch it or squeeze it too much. You may need to reinforce the joint with a snake of clay around the base of the handle; smooth it into place. Like sagging lids, sagging handles can be propped up with newspaper.

FORMS BUILT FROM SLABS

Many wonderful shapes can be built out of slabs of clay that are rolled, cut out, scored, and stuck together. To roll a slab, place two 15-inch wood strips, each about ½ inch thick, on your canvas- or burlap-covered work surface. The strips should be close enough so that your rolling pin will rest on them at either end. This will ensure slabs of uniform thickness. Slice off a piece of clay, 1 to 3 inches thick, and bang it on the table to flatten it before rolling. Place it between the wood strips and roll away, making sure the rolling pin stays on top of the wood strips at either end. Roll in several directions to present prevent cracking.

SIZE

What you wish to make, the size of your kiln, and the kind of clay you will be using will determine the size of your slab. A thickness of at least ½ inch is recommended, though thinner pieces may work. Again, optimal thickness depends on the type of clay, so find out as much as you can from your dealer to ensure that your pieces are fired safely.

TEXTURE

A wide variety of objects can be pressed into clay, either before or after assembling the slabs, but be aware that pressing will slightly distort edges. Try objects such as pine needles, fern leaves, or sheets of texture like screening or lace. Lay them out on top of the slab. Then, firmly run the rolling pin across the slab to impress but not embed the objects. Texture can even be a substitute for color.

SHAPES

Cylinders, cones, and other round forms: Slabs can be rolled into cylinders and stood on end to become cups, vases, or bowls, or they can be used as cylindrical bases, like legs. Slabs can also be draped over wads of newspaper to create hollow cavelike shapes or turned over and used as convex shapes for masks or landscapes (if propped with crumpled newspaper). Slabs can even be rolled into cones for volcanoes, or beehives, or tree trunks. An upside-down pinch pot can be placed on the trunk and cut and modeled to form leaves.

Squares, rectangles, and triangles: Slabs in these shapes can be fitted together to make box forms. To ensure matching sides, templates can be cut out of tagboard or heavy paper, but many children prefer to make boxes just by measuring the pieces against each other. These forms have an irregular charm that is quite individual.

When the pieces are cut out, score the edges of the base and sides. As they are assembled, lay little snakes of clay along the inner seams and smooth the snakes into place. The outside seam should also be smoothed by pushing clay from one joined piece to another—not by running a finger along the seam and thus weakening it.

Lids for boxes are fashioned in the same way as for pinch pots. When handles are attached, they must be secured as described earlier in this chapter.

Once a box (a "house") is made, two slabs can be propped against each other to make a roof. Triangles can be fitted into place on the front and back of the roof, or it can be left open. If newspaper is used inside for propping the roof, make sure the front door is big enough to remove it before firing. (Although newspaper will vaporize during firing, burning newspaper is not really good for the kiln and the quick fire can create a hot spot that cracks the pot.)

In the same way, triangles can be assembled into pyramids. We have had them made out of both three and four sides in our classes.

Tiles: Tiles can be cut from slabs to be used individually or put into a larger piece. Individual tiles can be hung by poking a hole about ¾ inch from the top of the tile. To prevent warping, score the backs of the tiles with a cross from end to end.

Most children will not make a conscious decision about the outside shape of their tile unless you bring it to their attention. Do you want it square or round? It is important to point out that this is part of their piece and this is a decision to be made. If you are working with a large group, you can give each child a 6-inch template and have them all cut a tile the same size to facilitate beginnings. Unless you dictate the subject matter, you will find much individuality in treatment of the 6-inch space. Interesting shapes can also happen accidently while rolling and can be consciously used. This use of the unexpected or accidental is part of the essence of making art and should be pointed out to young artists. Once, I rolled out a shape that looked like the face of a friend with a beard, so that's what it became. I don't think I could have done it on purpose!

You can also build fairly large shapes on tiles, working in what is called high relief. If shapes get too thick, they can be hollowed out from behind. Both building and carving should be tried. Older children can let their tiles dry and then carve details and refine roughness when leather-hard, without distorting the form.

Nature tiles are also popular. Grasses, thick leaves or small branches with pods, seashells, and so on are pressed into the clay. If you can, let the children gather and bring in their own materials.

The need for holiday art can take the form of tiles for Valentine's Day or other celebrations. Pre-patterned shapes should be avoided. As long as choice is offered and personal expression and workmanship are emphasized, tiles can be very exciting.

They also lend themselves to group projects. In this case, cut 4-inch tiles and suggest that each child make a symbol of something he or she associates with himself or herself. Later, the group's tiles can be assembled around a door frame, on an outside wall, or on a room divider. Four-inch tiles can be

Top left: Creating texture with an everyday object. Top right: Scoring. Center left: Slabs for boxes are cut using a pattern. Center right: After attaching strip stops that will hold the lid firmly in place, the handle is hollowed slightly. Bottom left: Newspaper packed into the box will prevent the lid from sagging during drying. Bottom right: Remove newspaper from the finished piece before firing.

Mua, age 14, made this "Artist Shrine" after being inspired by Dia de Los Muertos art of Mexico.

attached with waterproof glue to a four-by-four or mounted with Scotch Squares to a plywood backing before being mounted on the wall.

Just remember: A load of tiles takes more room to fire than a mixed load.

Making bases: All sorts of regularly and irregularly shaped slabs can be used as bases for ceramic pieces. The bases can be permanently attached or removable. They do not have to be flat; they can be folded and draped over the other shapes to dry.

Sculptured landscapes or scenes containing different objects or creatures are consistently popular. One girl created a scene from the San Diego Zoo, which she had visited when the panda was on loan from China. It included the panda, trees, and herself photographing the panda with a tiny clay camera. Older children have made scenes from books they have read. To illustrate *The Pearl*, by John Steinbeck, one boy made a scene with beach, waves, and a man in a rowboat. A girl made a replica of an ancient temple by looking at a picture in her history book and using slabs on a slab base. Scenes may also be purely imaginative, thus incorporating the propitious accident. After one little girl made a landscape, she noticed that the animal was as big as the tree. I could see her mind work as she looked back and forth from animal to tree, finally saying, "It's a dinosaur." Later she added more land and made a fabulous dinosaurscape.

There is something very appealing about making landscapes. The opportunity to make order out of this confusing world is one of art's most satisfying aspects.

Creating strips and other shapes: Slabs can be cut into strips for construction or added on to tiles, boxes, and bowls as relief elements. Older children can weave them and drape them over a bowl to dry, or braid or twist them.

RESPECT FOR UNIQUE EXPRESSIONS

I cannot emphasize enough how different each child is and, thus, how different their goals are. They will run the gamut from creating utilitarian objects to making abstract and gestural statements, to just spending lots of time working with a malleable material without making anything. These differences must be respected; our role as teachers is simply to help them make their pieces so that they hold together and to draw their attention to what they are doing on their own. Giving them lots of time to work is important, because the process has its own meaning. For most children, however, the end product is still the mark of accomplishment.

KILNS AND KILN FURNITURE

Your work will need two firings: a bisque firing and a glaze firing. It's certainly advantageous to be able to do this yourself if you're going to hold regular clay sessions. Look into the cost of a kiln. It will not be astronomical. (Electric kilns have the least safety requirements. They run on 220 wiring, just as an oven or clothes dryer does.) Many public schools have kilns, though they may be hidden away in the custodian's utility room or in a boiler-room. Used kilns became available when people move or change their plans.

If you find yourself able to make use of a kiln, discuss its operation with an experienced person. The dealer should come to your school to show you how to operate a new kiln. If there is not an experienced person nearby, be sure to read the kiln manual thoroughly. I found my manual intelligible even without the help of a teenager.

Determine what cones (little slivers of clay that stand on end and droop at a certain temperature; the drooping either shuts off the kiln automatically or signals the operator to turn it off) your kiln is capable of firing at, whether it has a timer, a kiln sitter (a cone-activated, mechanical device to shut off the kiln at the proper temperature), and what the manufacturer's dos and don'ts are. You can also find out a lot from your local supplier of clay and glazes. It is crucial to know what type of clay you will be using and at what cone it should be fired.

You should have an assortment of kiln furniture, which consists of shelves and posts. Your dealer can recommend furniture for a kiln of the size you have. I keep a shelf on the bottom of the kiln at all times, to protect it. Half shelves are great—they provide flexibility in loading.

BISQUE FIRING

PRELIMINARIES TO FIRING

Examine used shelves for chipped kiln wash, the white substance they are coated with. Chipped shelves and new, uncoated shelves should be brushed with kiln wash, which is bought as a white powder and mixed with water.

If you have a kiln sitter, you must put the cone in place prior to loading. The kiln will not turn on without the trigger switch being in position, and its position is controlled by the cone. After carefully loading the kiln and congratulating yourself on fitting everything in, discovering you have forgotten the cone is very annoying.

LOADING

The sides of the kiln are of firebrick. Be careful as you load—do not knock the sides with a heavy shelf. The brick chips easily and, over time, electric elements may be exposed. The lower part of the kiln is the cooler part. Place lighter-weight pieces on the bottom. Unglazed clay can be placed close to and even touching other unglazed clay pieces. But, since firing can be affected by circulation around pieces, it's best not to pack loads too tightly. If you must fire very full loads, make sure to compensate by firing well-dried pieces only.

Arranging the pieces is a skill that improves with practice. It's like loading the trunk of a car. By trial and error, you will find the arrangement of posts and shelves best suited to your ceramics. You will build layers of shelves from the bottom up, using three or four posts of the same height to support the shelves. Each time you set down a shelf, test it for stability. Does it rock or teeter? Suppose the heavy lid slips from your hand when you are shutting the kiln and falls with a thud. Could your shelves withstand the jarring? Make sure no ceramic piece is taller than or the same height as the space between shelves (you don't want a shelf resting on fragile clay). Tall, unglazed pieces can be laid on their sides in a bisque fire.

FIRING

All the kilns that I have worked with have been electric kilns with kiln sitters. The firing times I will mention in this section are based on this experience. Timing for other kinds of kilns differs—you will have to get to know your own kiln so that you can use it with as much confidence as possible. I've learned by doing, which has included making mistakes. But don't worry—if you've roasted a Thanksgiving turkey, you can run a kiln. Clay should be thoroughly dry. When clay is dry, it changes color and is lighter in weight than when wet. Knowing if the inside is dry is impossible, but you shouldn't be firing anything thicker than 1 inch. Clay that looks and feels dry will be fired to the appropriate cone after 5 to 6 hours. If your kiln has an automatic shutoff, check on the timing by being there when the kiln shuts off. If you do not have an automatic shutoff, you will be looking through a peephole in the side of the kiln to see when the cone melts, which means it's time to turn off the kiln.

I use clays that fire to cone .04 or .05. Start on low with the kiln lid propped open a few inches, for moisture to escape, and with all the peepholes

open. Your kiln will include cone-shaped plugs that fit into these holes when they are needed. I fire on low for a minimum of 1 hour, on medium for 1 hour, on high for ½ hour, and then I close the lid. Place plugs in at least two of the three peepholes, and leave the kiln on high until it is time to turn it off. The gradual heating allows the drying process to finish slowly. If clay dries too fast, it will crack. By closing the lid after the kiln has been on high for a while, you will avoid a sudden increase in temperature.

If you are in a hurry and your clay isn't quite dry, leather-hard clay can be "candled." Turn one of the switches on to low (there are usually two switches for each setting) in the late afternoon or evening, and leave the kiln on overnight. Turn the second "low" switch on in the morning. If you are in doubt, you may want to leave the switch on low and medium longer than usual. A handy way to help ceramic work to dry gradually is to store it on shelves in the kiln room. The room will gradually warm when the kiln is being fired.

Your kiln's firing time and temperature can be checked by setting a cone upright on a shelf in front of a peephole and noting when it melts. If you suspect your clay or glazes are being over- or underfired, you will want to check this out. There is a possibility, even with a kiln that has an automatic timer, of overfiring. This means the kiln keeps getting hotter and hotter until it reaches its maximum—and your clay may melt in the process. It is

best to be there when you expect the kiln to turn off, just to make sure it does.

To prevent overfiring, make sure your timer is set to the correct number of hours. After being turned to high and with the lid shut, you should observe and record how long your kiln runs before it shuts off. If it runs for 3 hours before reaching the correct temperature and shutting off, then make sure your timer is set at 3 to 4 hours when you switch the kiln to high and leave to do other things. Don't go off and leave the timer set at 20 hours! Second, make sure you have loaded the kiln so that nothing is too close to the cone–actuating rod setup. The rod is the piece that rests on top of the cone on the kiln sitter. When the kiln reaches the proper temperature, the cone melts and the rod drops to release the trigger switch, which shuts off the power. Keep shelves and ceramic pieces clear of the cone and rod by about 1 inch. It's possible that a shelf closer than ½ inch could shift a bit as weight is added on top.

Another way to prevent overfiring is to make a traditional clay kiln god to watch over your firing. Since the only time I used a god was the only time the kiln overfired, I have decided that my kiln is an atheist, or at least that gods help those who set their timers properly.

Above left: Rashida Mead displays her ceramic bird, a slab construction that will hang on the wall. Below: "Portrait of Bronwyn Parks" was a gift to Rashida by friend Ariana Schoellhorn.

GLAZING YOUR CERAMICS

TIME The time required varies depending on the amount of work—three coats of glaze will be applied.

MATERIALS A variety of brushes—soft and firm, large and small

A set of sample tiles (see the explanation that follows)

An assortment of approved glaze colors (Glazes are made of a variety of compounds. Some of the best have been banned for use with children because of lead or other toxins. Some glazes are "food safe," which means you can eat off them after they are fired.)

Optional: Black or red iron oxide; paper, to rest pieces on while glazing; sponges

---

The second firing, the glaze firing, should be done at a temperature one or two cones cooler than the bisque firing. Most of the shrinkage will take place in the hotter firing (before the glaze is on). This avoids cracking in the glaze (moisture escaping the clay during shrinkage can cause the glaze to bubble). Another good reason not to skip the bisque firing is that the clay is so fragile without it—the handling required to apply the glaze may break the piece. Unless you have an unlimited number of bottles of glaze and brushes, you'll probably want to have only six or seven students, at most, working at the same time.

DOING IT Ask your glaze retailer about what glazes are approved for use with kindergartners through sixth graders. Once you have located a local source of approved glazes, you will find that you are working with a limited palette. Check as many resources as you can—quality varies greatly. For example, there is no approved opaque red, which is probably the most requested color in my classes. Other popular colors may also come only in transparent form, necessitating thorough application of at least three coats. Basic opaque colors are generally available. You may also choose matte or gloss finishes.

When buying glaze for a group, aim to provide at least black, white, clear, the primaries, and the secondaries (after firing). They look quite different in liquid form, and it requires a stretch of the imagination and a leap of faith on the part of the students to exercise some control over the results. To assist them to work intelligently, I make a set of sample tiles—a small one for each color, with the number of the glaze. I also show them finished pieces, which illustrate how the glaze colors change in the hot kiln.

It's not a bad idea to discuss color and contrast—not by giving an extended lecture, but by showing how different a piece of yellow paper looks on a white background than on dark blue, for example. Encourage students to check out all the available colors and play with the sample tiles, trying combinations instead of just slathering on any colors. Designs can be painted on simple forms. Dots, dribbles, and stripes enhance smooth surfaces or emphasize sculptural ones. Colors can also be applied on top of each other. Transparent colors will "mix" and make a new color. Light colors on top of dark colors combine in a similar way; darks on lights will probably not change. Glazes of the same brand can be mixed together with some success. Experiment.

Applying the glaze: Children may need some

encouragement here, so having some examples of finished work is helpful. Bottles of glaze should be thoroughly shaken and/or stirred before use. Clays vary in their textures; some are easier to glaze than others, but all require three coats to reveal color. It's fine to leave some areas unglazed, especially if you are using a clay whose color complements the glazes, but it should be done on purpose. Otherwise, glaze should be applied thickly by using soft-bristle brushes, taking care not to skip over parts and leave accidental pockmarks.

Fine lines can be brought out and emphasized by painting them with a mixture of black or red iron oxide and water. You can buy a small sack of this powder at the ceramics shop and mix it into paintable liquid. After it's dry, cover it with a coat of transparent glaze for a glossy finish, or leave it as is and paint around it to create very dark, matte lines.

In the kiln, glazed surfaces that come into contact with anything will melt in the heat and stick to the object against which they are resting. You have a choice of not glazing the bottom of your piece or glazing it and carefully setting it up on stilts. Stilts are stands with tiny points for the ceramics to sit on. They come in all sizes. The extra height they add to each piece will take up a bit more room in the kiln. Loading will also take more time if using stilts, especially when firing work that doesn't have a flat base. If you plan to fire this way, make sure to have stilts of many sizes and shapes.

I use stilts occasionally, for things like pot lids. Generally, however, I ask the students not to glaze the bottom of their work, and it usually doesn't make a difference aesthetically. To avoid accidentally painting the bottom, keep each piece on a separate sheet of paper. Turn the paper as you glaze and don't pick up the piece at all. If some glaze gets on the bottom, it can easily be sponged off.

Students will do a better glazing job if they understand the process of firing and why certain precautions are needed. Take them on a "field trip" to the kiln when it's not running. Tell them how hot it gets and that they can get burned just by touching the outside of it. Show them the shelves—maybe you have some marked by gobs of molten glaze. Your instructions will make much more sense if your students are informed about the process.

Do not fire work that is carelessly finished. It requires lots of human and electrical energy.

FIRING GLAZED WARE

Loading the kiln: When loading glazed pieces, make sure that the bottoms of each piece are free of glaze, or else set them on stilts. They should not touch each other or anything else. Make sure the shelves do not rest on top or touch anything that is glazed. Should anything stick to a shelf, a coat of kiln wash will protect the shelf but will mar the ceramic piece.

I put the tallest pieces on the very top of the load so that I don't have to build shelves up over them. You don't want shelves that wobble.

You may find that, once in a while, you will need to fire a mixed load of glazed and unglazed ware. Make sure you put the previously unfired pieces on the bottom. Then, should they explode, which does happen occasionally, bits of clay won't be sprayed onto glazed ware below.

Firing: Allow one day to fire and one day to cool pieces before unloading the kiln. You will fire your glazed ware at a lower temperature than the bisque fire. I use .06 cone for glaze firing. I begin by firing the glazes on low for an hour, with the kiln lid propped open a few inches and all peephole plugs removed to let glaze fumes out. (Although approved glazes should not emit toxic fumes, my ceramics dealer tells me it's easier on the kiln walls to vent the kiln by leaving holes open.) I finish off by firing on medium for another hour, turning the temperature to high, closing the lid, and replacing two or all three plugs after half an hour.

Glazed ware should be left in the kiln in order to cool to room temperature. If it cools too quickly, it may crack.

If glazed ware accidently sticks to another piece or a post during firing, it can usually be broken apart, and the rough part can be smoothed with the use of a metal file.

Ceramics that are underfired, glazed too thinly, or for which a different color is desired may be refired or reglazed and refired.

PLASTER

TIME One 20-minute session. Product will have to wait several hours to be dry enough to take home. In a large class, several students at a time can make molds, and plaster can be poured all at once later; if students can't help pour, at least let them watch!

MATERIALS Clay or sand for molds

Containers: Styrofoam trays; shoe boxes; candy or stationery boxes; plastic ice cream tubs, one-gallon size; tofu or other plastic food containers of all sizes

Plaster of paris: A 20-pound sack is quite inexpensive and will make about fifty projects, depending on size. Smaller amounts are available, but may cost just as much. Plaster can be found at hardware and building-supply stores.

Paper clips or hairpins to serve as hooks, for hanging the pieces

Clay tools and all texture-making tools listed in the preceding chapter, "Clay"

Shells, pods, wood, and other materials from nature

Newspapers

Large, flexible plastic mixing bowl

Water, to mix plaster

Mixing spoon

Dust masks to prevent inhaling plaster particles (if students mix their own plaster)

Optional: Disposable cup, for transferring plaster; paint, acrylic or other water-based; aluminum foil; plastic wrap; toothpick; background material; glue; paintbrush; linseed oil; miscellaneous materials for sculptures (see "Other Projects," later in this chapter)

DOING IT Choose a container for your work. Take a big piece of clay (can be old used clay), flatten it, and roll it out to form a slab. Put the container, right side up, on top of the slab and trim around the bottom edge (so the clay will fit in the bottom of the container). At least ½ inch should be left between the clay and the rim of the container for pouring plaster.

Removing hardened plaster from a clay mold.

Put the clay in the container. Run your fingers along edge of the clay to seal it to the side of the container. Remember, all the marks you make in the clay will be picked up by the plaster. The edge may be pressed in a decorative way while sealing, or simply smoothed. Press tools or objects into the clay or remove clay to form a design. Press deeply enough for the impression to show clearly. If a child wants to press very deeply, he or she should have a piece of clay that is thick enough. The wrong end of a paintbrush makes an effective drawing tool.

Each element of the design will be reversed when cast in plaster. Warn those who want to include words to write them backwards.

When the design is finished, attach a piece of tape with the artist's name to the container at the top edge of the design. You will then know where to place the hook after the plaster is poured and covers the design.

Mixing the plaster: Cover a table with newspapers and ventilate the room. If students are to do the mixing, have them wear protective masks. A large volume of dry plaster is needed in proportion to water: 1 to 2 parts plaster to 1 part water. You can use warm water for a quicker set. To mix, proceed as follows: Pour the water into the plastic bowl. One cup at a time, gently "salt" plaster onto the water. Do not stir. Do not drop the plaster, in one lump, into the water. Keep salting, cup by cup, until the level of the plaster is just under the top of the water—don't stir until it reaches this level. Then stir gently; it should feel like cake batter or heavy cream, and it shouldn't be runny. Keep the stirring to a minimum to avoid introducing a lot of air bubbles into the mixture.

If you have made a big batch of plaster for several containers, use a disposable cup to dip into the mixture and fill them. Young people love to fill their own molds. Have a bucket of water available for them to rinse their hands rather than using the sink (plaster is not good for plumbing). Fill molds with a layer of plaster from ½ inch to 1 inch thick. In warm weather, plaster may start to set immediately, so be prepared to place your hook—an opened paper clip or hairpin—near the top of the piece. Place it mostly in the plaster, but leave enough out to hang on a nail.

Wait at least several hours to unmold the pieces. Plaster will warm up as it is setting. Before unmolding, it should be cool, but can still be damp. In fact, avoid letting the clay get dry underneath or it will not lift off the plaster. You will share in the children's excitement as they pull away the clay to reveal creations that are always beautiful and fascinating. This is a project that never fails.

Some plaster pieces have the look of fossils. Others can be richly detailed sculptural reliefs in plain white, playing with light and shadow. After you rinse off excess clay, the pieces can be painted with acrylics or water-based paints. Crumpled aluminum foil or smooth plastic wrap lining a container will produce a wonderfully wrinkled casting or one as smooth as glass. Plaster picks up and reproduces the tiniest detail in everything from wood grains to fabric.

Allow the plaster to dry in your bowl and spoon. Later, it can be flaked off by scraping the spoon and

Pariscraft or surgical bandage is an exciting medium for older children creating plaster sculptures. Use stuffed bags or chicken wire armatures for support.

bending and slightly twisting the bowl. Make sure not to wash any liquid plaster down the sink.

SAND CASTING

Put a layer of damp or dry sand at least 1 inch thick in a shoe box or other container. Press shells, pods, driftwood, and so on firmly into the sand, remembering that the side now facing you will be covered with plaster—it is the side pressed into the sand that will show. Virtually anything—from bottle lids to nuts and bolts—can be used, but the finished casting will have a fine coating of sand that seems more suitable to natural objects. Mix and pour plaster and proceed as above. Sand, like clay, can be reused for future castings.

OTHER PROJECTS

You can make little objects in a thick piece of clay without a container. For that matter, if you don't have a container, you can make walls of clay scored all around and stuck onto a bottom slab. For individual small pieces, experimenting will show best what works. Start with something simple, like pressing a large spoon deeply to create a depression that will hold plaster. This can be made into a face or any design you like. Stick a toothpick in near the top to make a hole if you want to hang the piece by

string. (Remove the toothpick when the plaster sets up.) When these pieces are cast, they will be raised on one side and flat on the other. They can be glued on a background, painted, or otherwise decorated.

Children's enthusiasm can also lead to much larger projects. We have built clay molds around hands and feet—then carefully wriggled out and poured in the plaster. Clay should be removed from these freestanding molds while it is still moist, but after the plaster has set. (To keep the clay moist, you can put the whole thing inside a plastic bag; the plaster will still continue to set while in the bag.)

Plaster castings can be displayed outside. They hold up very well naturally, but for longer life, coat them with three or four layers of linseed oil.

Plaster can be carved with a dull knife, the edge of scissors, a paper clip, a ruler, or just about any straight edge, or it can be filed when damp, a capability that increases its possible uses—especially for older children.

It can be used to make full-scale sculptures by building armatures of wire or cardboard or using plastic bags stuffed with paper and shaped. Muslin dipped in plaster is layed on the armatures to dry. We have used surgical bandage and Pariscraft, both expensive—but they are easy to use because you dip plaster-saturated cloth in water rather than dipping a dry cloth in wet plaster, a tricky and drippy process. Look at figure sculptor Manuel Neri's work for inspiration.

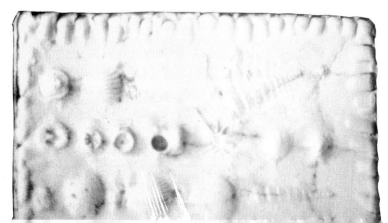

8

PUPPETS

He hasn't named me yet. I'm an alien. I'm from Planet Punk. Everyone who lives there is a punk. It's weird. I don't like it—that's why I came here. My name is Spike. My tail keeps me warm at night. I'm a private eye. I solve mysteries. I have one gold medal for doing five mysteries. After five mysteries you get a gold medal. I'm going to go to Dustin's house; he has a very bad problem and I'm going to help him solve it.

—Dustin, age seven

I'm about six and a half. I have a mohawk. I like to go bowling. I like to play with my hair. I like living in Sebastopol except in the winter, when I go to Idaho. I got in trouble in papier-mâché and I got nine hundred spankings. I felt so mad I bit the principal. Then he killed me and put me in the graveyard. Then I bit him again. Then he bit me again. I have a bruise on my forehead from the principal. I will spank him nine hundred times when I'm done with school.

—Graham, age six and a half

Puppet making opens children's imaginations and allows them to play out fantasies, enabling them to carry on the essential process of learning who they are, and how they fit in the world with others.

THE NEWSPAPER METHOD

TIME One or two papier-mâché sessions (15 to 30 minutes each); two sessions for painting, sewing, and decorating

MATERIALS Wheat paste (any of the following three can be used):

Wallpaper paste: Buy this paste from a hardware store or paint store.

Flour and water: Mix in flour until you achieve the consistency of pudding.

Cooked flour and water and white glue: Mix cold water with flour to form a puddinglike consistency. Bring the mixture to a slow boil, stirring constantly; simmer an hour or two. Throw in a squeeze of white glue somewhere along the line.

Containers for paste (Styrofoam food trays work well)

Materials for appendages: Cardboard egg cartons, paper cones, etc.

Newspapers: Black and white and colored, if possible

White paper towels: The stiff kind that you find at school

Rubber bands or string

Masking tape

Scissors

Toilet-paper rolls cut in half (one half per child)

Pins

Paints: Tempera or student-grade acrylic, such as Chromacryl

Paintbrushes

Fabric pieces, each no smaller then 12 inches square; a wide variety

Decorations: Buttons, beads, etc.

Optional: Oil of wintergreen (a few drops in the paste improves the smell)

Balloons

Sewing machine

Pattern, for costume

Thick needles

Felt (for hands)

Pop or beer bottles, the tall kind, half filled with sand

Polyurethane coating

DOING IT Break up large classes into groups of six or seven children, each group working with one adult. It is useful to have an extra adult around to help with sewing.

Cover your tables. Tear a sheet of newspaper in half, then tear each half in half. Crumple the larger sheet into a ball about the size of an orange. Place the ball in the center of the quarter sheet. Bring the four corners together around the ball like a lollipop.

The toilet-paper roll will serve as the neck. Put the stem of the newspaper "lollipop" through the paper roll and tape the neck to the ball, or head. If

Starting to apply the papier-mâché is the hardest part for young children. Once the first few pieces are on, it's much easier to work with. Some children learn primarily by watching other children.

using a bottle, push the newspaper stem to one side and slip the neck over the bottle top. Using a bottle allows the puppet maker's hands to work on all sides, and the puppet head to dry when finished.

Now you can tape shapes to the head for features: eyes, ears, snouts, trunks, and so on. Use pieces cut out of cardboard egg cartons; paper cones; and bent, folded, or twisted newspaper. You can dip paper into paste to help shape it.

For those who want to make very large puppet heads, use small balloons rather than newspaper balls. Necks and other features can be taped to the balloons in the same way as to the newspaper forms. A balloon-based head is rigid and doesn't have quite the modeling possibilities of newspaper, but a really large head can get awfully heavy if it isn't hollow.

Apply papier-mâché: Tear sheets of black-and-white newspaper lengthwise to create strips. Make the strips fairly small—this is a small project. If you have access to solid-colored newspaper, make a separate pile for strips of colored paper. Make a third pile of strips made from the white paper

towels. Three layers of strips are just about perfect for creating a strong puppet head. And by changing colors for each layer, students can keep track of the layers. Use the white strips for the last layer. The white layer results in a better surface for painting since the paint color won't have to compete with the paper color.

It seems the world is divided into two kinds of people: those who loathe touching gooey stuff and those who revel in squeezing stuff like papier-mâché paste through their fingers. The "dry" people will have to be encouraged to rub on enough paste to get that first layer to stay down, and the "wet" people will have to be reminded to remove excess paste if they want their puppet to dry within their lifetimes. The dry people will complain or make faces, but they always seem to make it through the terrible torture and usually become the most enthusiastic painters and decorators. Some of the wet people will continue to add layer upon layer, quietly humming away to themselves while you don't notice, until their puppet is so heavy you

can barely pick it up. Try to get these types to strike some sort of balance. To get the right amount of paste, run strips through paste and then through two fingers to remove excess.

Make sure to attach the head to the neck securely with lengthwise strips. Added-on features should be fastened in the same way.

Don't attach the neck to the bottle with papier-mâché. It's hard to get off later and takes too long to dry that way. Tape it, if you want security.

Drying the papier-mâché: Paper-mâché will take from one to several days to dry. You can speed up the drying process by putting work in the sun. Prop up large, extended features, such as elephant trunks or open beaks. When the head is dry, pull out the stuffing if you can. This is not necessary, but it can be lots of fun.

Painting the puppets: You are now ready to paint the head. Provide three or four sizes of fairly stiff bristle brushes. (Don't use watercolor brushes with acrylics; the brushes are too soft.) I use student-grade acrylic paint because it provides a permanent finish. Acrylics cover much more area than tempera or watercolor paints, so squeeze out small amounts at first. A tablespoon or two will cover an entire head. Children need to be shown that this paint is different than tempera and needs to be brushed out. Tempera paint can also be used and later sprayed with polyurethane.

Making the costumes: After the paint is dry, ask the students to select pieces of fabric for the front and back of costumes. For those who don't want to sew, cut a circle with a smaller circle in the center for the neck. For sewing, make a simple pattern with sleeves and about a 3-inch neck opening. Cut out the fabric and pin the right sides together. Hand- or machine-sew side seams. You can leave sleeves open—children's fingertips make nice puppet hands. Alternately, you can sew sleeves closed or, later, add felt "hands." A puppet costume is a very appropriate sewing project for those using the machine for the first time. Please see the fabric chapter for tips on sewing with children.

To attach the costume, hold the puppet head for the puppet maker and have him or her dab a thick coat of white glue around the base of the neck—a ½-inch band. Bunch up the costume like a sock, then back it up to the head rather than slipping it over—in other words, place the neck of the costume along the edge of the neck, with the right side of the fabric along the glue. With the fabric bunched around the head, adjust the neck edge. Make sure the side seams of the costume are lined up properly with the head, then press the fabric into the glue. Place a rubber band or tie a string around the neck until the glue dries.

Any manner of finery can be added now. Buttons, beads, broken jewelry, feathers, fur, yarn—it's up to the imagination.

THE MODELING-CLAY METHOD

TIME Three or four sessions with two drying periods in between. One hour or two half-hour sessions to model heads and apply papier-mâché, followed by a drying period; a 15-minute session to cut open heads, remove clay, and re-paste. Allow to dry again and then have a 15- to 30-minute session to paint and decorate the puppets.

MATERIALS Same as for the newspaper method

Modeling clay (Plasticine)

Exacto knife

Long knife

This project is for older children (over nine) and should be done only in small groups. The removing of clay needs to be directly supervised and the cutting done by an adult with an Exacto knife. Hasty removal can cause tears in the papier-mâché, rendering an entire period's work useless.

DOING IT Older children can model puppets from Plasticine, an oil-based, nondrying "clay" found at toy and art-supply stores. (Large amounts may be scarce, but college art-supply stores may stock it for sculpture classes. It is not cheap, but is reusable.) It's important that the clay be pliable. If it is cold, it will be hard to model. Putting it in the sun or a low oven will help (but if you do this, watch it carefully).

The advantage of modeling clay is that finer and more "realistic" features can be modeled, and changes are easy to make because of its flexibility. Be sure that a neck is included. We all have a vague idea about how necks connect to heads, but looking in a mirror will help students solidify their impressions. Positioning can make the difference between the head looking like a human's or an animal's.

Three layers of papier-mâché will be applied to the head, as in the other puppet-making process. If a child's modeling-clay head has small features, the student will need to tear paper into small pieces to fit over, around, and in and out of the head's hills and valleys. After the papier-mâché is hard and dry, you should cut it in half with an Exacto knife or other sharp tool. Then cut through the clay with a long knife, and pull the head apart. The children can remove the clay, put the heads back together with small bits of masking tape, then papier-mâché along the seam. (This extra step makes this way of working take too long for younger children.)

ADDITIONAL ADVICE

Young children like to splotch colors over their puppets' heads and enjoy mixing and smearing colors. It's hard for children to see the value of painting a base coat and letting it dry before adding painted features. I never force them until they are ready to move from one stage to another. However,

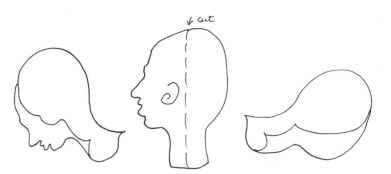

When using the modeling-clay method, cut in half laterally rather than down the center of the face.

I do discuss this idea and ask them to decide what kind of creature they are making, what color skin or fur it has. I also talk about how contrast makes things visible—showing examples more than talking. Ask the children to note that puppets on stage are seen from a distance and thus should have exaggerated features and bright, high-contrast colors. Some children may be interested in putting on a puppet show. With a small group of children, you might try making characters from a favorite book and then let their imaginations rewrite the story.

Other children simply make little friends or alter egos or pets they are not allowed to have. Try to tune in to what they are after. Even if they don't care about the theatrical aspects of puppets, all but the very young appreciate tips on how to make their creatures look more like what they have in mind (not the teacher's idea of what that might be). Talk about eyes not just being black dots (human and some animal eyes have quite a bit of white showing) and point out that lips aren't really red but just darker skin color. We can point these and similar things out but, in the end, what each student does with this information should be under his or her control. If young people cannot ever realize their own ideas of how things are, they will eventually not bother to try.

The photos on pages 62 and 63 illustrate a series of puppet creations made over a period of five years by two students from ages six to eleven. The increase in skill is obvious, but the development of the personal content and style is even more interesting. Mua repeats the cat theme with increasing sophistication. Megan's little girls with braids give way to elegantly dressed animals: a cat, bear, dog, and "Spanish mouse." Freedom of expression was an essential element of such wonderful progress.

9

MASKS

My mask is pretty. It is my face. It has mostly purple on it. I showed it to my mom. I popped the balloon. It has a little red on it. I painted it. I'm going to wear it to play. It feels hard now, but it was soft when I was making it. I put on a double-pink bead, and some shells, and a fur mouth. And fur hair. And a swirly bead, glitter, and a paddle-wheel bead. It feels good on me.

—Carly, age five

I made it with papier-mâché. It is black with lots of other colors, orange, and skin color. It's a rainbow cheetah. It likes to have lots of colors on it when it runs. It likes to eat zebras and snakes and plants. It gets a haircut every week. It's pretty. I liked popping the balloon.

—Ananda, age eight

Mask making is very popular with all ages. It allows the artist to give expression to the inner self or explore other potential personalities without criticism. Often, children's masks are familiar creatures—loved and admired animals or humans. Some will make masks that are timeless, mythic creatures: the wise man, the devil, the warrior. Making such frightening creatures in solid form gives the child the chance to play with that fear and other powerful feelings and forces within that can overwhelm young people.

At your local library, look up books on "primitive" societies, consult magazines such as *National Geographic,* or borrow some of the excellent children's magazines like *Ranger Rick* to find pictures of masks *in use* among the indigenous peoples of North America, the Amazon, Mexico, or Africa. The masks of ancient cultures are exciting and inspiring to children who have seen only plastic Halloween masks. Showing actual masks is, of course, even better than photographs. Explore local ethnic shops or museums. Here you can purchase contemporary papier-mâché versions of old and still-exciting images. Remember, children will imitate examples, so show them good ones!

This chapter will present three different ways to make masks: the balloon method, which is the easiest and best-known option; the clay-mold method, which is slightly more involved; and a way to make life masks, which is best attempted by older children since it requires being still and having one's face covered.

Masks can serve the purpose of embellishing, like Carly's, and extending a child's imaginative existence, like Ananda's, or can be used for role playing. The mask at left is meant to be the artist's dad.

THE BALLOON METHOD

TIME One to two papier-mâché sessions (15 to 30 minutes each); one to two sessions to paint and decorate

MATERIALS Newspapers: Black and white and colored, if possible

Papier-mâché paste (see Chapter 8, "Puppets," for alternatives)

Paste containers (Styrofoam trays work well)

Permanent marker

Paper towels (the stiff kind you find in school) or brown bags

Masking tape

Sturdy balloons (party-supply stores have good ones) or plastic or paper bags

Containers to hold balloons while working, one container per child: Gallon-sized plastic containers work well; plastic hospital basins are also great.

These keep balloons from wobbling while the artists work. In a pinch, you can tape the balloons to sturdy paper plates.

Cardboard egg cartons and other cardboard pieces

Scissors

Glue

Water to thin glue

Decorations: Paint (student-grade acrylic is best for a permanent finish, although tempera will do fine and can be coated with a sealer), yarn, feathers, beads, buttons, tissue paper, etc.

Optional: Needle and thread, colored tissue paper

Let children work in small groups of six or seven at large work tables. Adult guidance is needed.

DOING IT Cover your table with newspapers. If using a balloon, inflate it and tie it *securely*. Use a permanent marker to draw a line that divides the balloon into front and back. (You can also write the artist's name on the back of the balloon.) Place each balloon in a container or tape it to a plate. If using bags, stuff them with newspaper and tie each one at the bottom. Then continue as with balloons.

The students can tear up fairly large pieces of newspaper. If your local paper has colored sections, use it to make a separate pile of pink or whatever color your paper's section may be. Make a third pile

from torn pieces of paper towel or brown bags. These pieces will become the final layer of papier-mâché. You can also experiment with colored butcher papers or plain newsprint for the final layer. Changing colors of layers helps students know when a layer has been covered completely, and ending with a plain paper facilitates painting.

Although appendages can be added later, it is preferable that noses, fangs, horns, and the like be taped to the balloon or bag before the papier-mâché process begins, especially when working with small children. These shapes can be torn from cardboard egg cartons, made from toilet-paper rolls or newspaper rolled into cones or folded into other shapes. Find the right location on the balloon before taping

down the appendage, because the balloon will surely pop if you try to pull off the tape to change the location.

Eye holes can be drawn on the balloon or bag and left open by not pasting paper over them. Or they can be cut out later. The space between human eyes is the size of an eye. An alternative to blank eyes is to paint the eyes on the mask and cut unnoticeable slits for the wearer to see out of. This allows the artist to have fun with the mask's eyes and enhances the mask's drama. (See examples of traditional African, Mexican, Chinese, and Balinese masks. Contemporary artists who work in this medium are the Linares family of Mexico.) After noses or other appendages have been attached, you are ready for the first layer of papier-mâché.

Applying the papier-mâché: Set the paste containers so that children can comfortably reach them. Show children how to put the newspaper strip in the paste and slide two fingers down the strip to remove excess paste.

Cover the whole mask with a first layer. (The first layer is the hardest because the balloon may wobble.) Help younger children to work inside the mask outline that you have drawn on the balloon. Turn it for them to see all sides.

If features have not been previously taped on, they can now be formed with wads of paper towels or newspaper that are first dipped in paste, modeled and shaped, and added to the mask after a layer of strips has been put down. Softened, wet paper can be modeled almost like clay.

If you have colored newsprint, use it to make your second layer or alternate paper towel or brown bag pieces with newspaper to make sure each layer is fully covered. There should be three complete layers in all. Four are okay, but more than four will be too heavy to wear comfortably.

It's easier but not necessary to do all three layers in one sitting. Depending on the weather, masks will dry in anywhere from a few hours to a few days. Put them in a sunny window or, in winter, near a

heat source. Avoid direct sun on a hot day since it can cause balloons to pop. If a balloon should pop for this or any other reason, it is often possible to remove it from under a still-wet mask and replace it by blowing up another balloon inside the mask.

Older children may experiment with putting all three layers of paper on at once. Spread paste on a piece of paper held in the palm of your hand, then slap on another piece of paper, more paste, and one final piece of paper. Apply all three pieces to the form. The mask is thus built in patches of layers.

When the masks are dry, the children can pop the balloons or cut the bags and pull out the stuffing. Any ragged edges can then be trimmed off of the masks.

Painting the mask: For details about painting, see Chapter 8, "Puppets." Offer a wide selection of different-sized paintbrushes, and have palettes nearby on which to mix colors to order. (If "skin color" is desired, mix your own rather than use what is sold as "peach," which is obviously too limited a choice.) Acrylic paint will not need any further protection. If using tempera paint, you can spray or paint the mask with varnish, or you can coat it with thinned white glue. Since tempera is water soluble, apply the glue delicately (it shouldn't be scrubbed on, or the paint will dissolve and smear). Glue dries transparently, with a slight sheen. Most children can coat their own masks.

Decorating the mask: After the paint is dry, decorative material can be glued on or attached with needle and thread. There is no end to possibilities: Apply yarn, hair, fur, feathers, whiskers, teeth, hats, beads, sequins, bits of fabric—whatever you can think of.

Another way to finish a mask is by applying colored tissue with thinned white glue. The paper is transparent, and colors will mix where overlapped. This technique creates a lovely polished look. Glue should be thinned until watery and brushed on the mask where the piece of paper is to be placed. Put down the paper and brush over it. Try adding several layers.

A LESSON IN PERSISTENCE

Younger children may need encouragement to persist through the application of three layers, but this persistence is very important. Sometimes younger children leave lots of ends sticking out—I try to get them to smooth these down without making it an obsession. Finishing this project is an eye-opener for children, because it is for many the first time they have experienced the fruits of real persistence and the transformation of homely, ordinary materials into art.

THE CLAY-MOLD METHOD

TIME One 30- to 45-minute session to make a mold, a few hours or days for the clay to harden, and one or two 30-minute sessions of papier-mâché

MATERIALS: Used clay is fine. Quantity is discussed later in this project. (No need to worry about wedging, because this clay will not be fired.)

Clay-working tools (see Chapter 6, "Clay," for suggestions)

Exacto knife

Vaseline

Newspapers or brown bags

Paper towels

Papier-mâché paste (see Chapter 8, "Puppets," for alternatives)

Decorations (see the preceding project for suggestions and means of attachment)

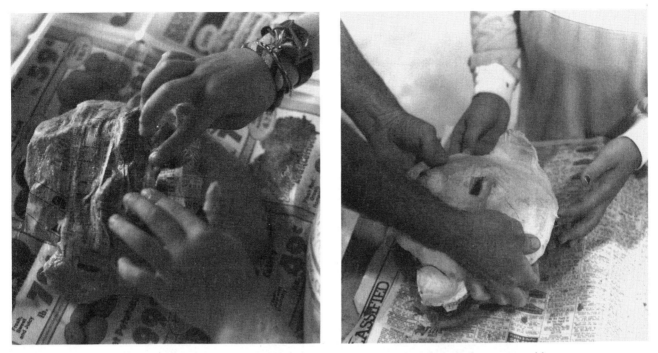

Making masks on clay molds allows an artist to create several masks from one mold.

A traditional way of making masks, the ceramic clay molds offer another chance to work with clay without needing a kiln.

DOING IT Help the children prepare the clay. Determine the size of the mask: Is it to be a full face or half a face? To fit the maker or decorate the wall? Average full-sized masks require a piece of clay 2 to 3 inches thick by 5 to 7 inches across. Round it out, hollowing out the back somewhat.

While you are making the big lumps of clay, have the children feel their faces and notice the hills and valleys. Let them look in a mirror to see where features are located. Then have them wad a couple of sheets of newspaper into a "pillow" for the mask mold to help keep it from flattening out.

As with all clay construction, parts that are added on must be firmly scored (see Chapter 6, "Clay"). Since the mask will be pulled off this mold, artists must stick the parts on really well. Pinching out shapes is preferable. For the same reason, there can be no undercuts in the modeling of the features. Noses, hooked shapes, and overhanging parts should be modeled so that they flare out at the bottom. Imagine what might catch and tear when pulled off a mold, and point this out to the students. Undercuts can be filled in by thumbing in

clay or wrapping snakes of clay around the bases of the offending feature. You may have to help a bit, but the student can certainly smooth the snakes into place and put on the final touches.

Many younger children will think the clay is the mask. The process may be incomprehensible until they see it completed, so have samples on hand.

When the clay is leather-hard, it is dry enough to work on. The molds need to be "greased" with Vaseline so that the papier-mâché mask will lift off. Check each mold to see if it is thoroughly greased. Have children clean their hands with paper towels; water will not remove Vaseline.

Now they can apply papier-mâché just as for balloon masks. When the paper is dry, an adult should cut around the outside edge of each mask with an Exacto knife. After putting the knife safely away, loosen the mask by running the handle of a spoon or fork under the mask edge. If eye holes have been left open, remove the mask by putting your thumbs on the eyes and lifting the mask off with your fingers. If eye holes have not been cut, pry gently all around. It seems like nothing is happening and then, suddenly, it's off!

Wipe away excess Vaseline with paper towels and decorate as discussed in the preceding section of this chapter, "The Balloon Method."

LIFE MASKS

TIME About 15 minutes of preparation time and about 10 minutes of actual molding time per child (each pair of children must be supervised by one adult), a 30-minute session for painting and decorating

MATERIALS
Quick-drying surgical bandage, 4 inches wide

Scissors

Newspaper

Felt-tip pen

Vaseline

Clean plastic bags

Pans of water

Paint (acrylic, tempera, or watercolor)

Decorations (see page 70 for suggestions)

DOING IT Children work in pairs for this project. Help them to make a pattern of each other's faces: Hold paper to the face and draw the outline. Gently feel for eye sockets and mouth and outline them. Locate the end of the nose and mark its position on the paper. Cut the pattern in half horizontally, just under the end of the nose. (The top half of the pattern will be from the hairline to the tip of the nose; the bottom half from the base of the nose, under the nostrils, to the bottom of the chin.) The nostril area will be left open for breathing. Use the pattern to cut out bandage pieces, two for the top and two for the bottom. Also, cut two ½-inch strips to place on the area between the nostrils.

Coat the child's face well with Vaseline, then pull a plastic bag over the hair. If you can monitor this closely, it is preferable to have the bag cover

Children can paint finished life masks as realistically or fantastically as they choose.

the eyes of younger children as they may blink. Never put the plastic bag over the nose and mouth.

You will need to help the partner apply the bandage: Dip a piece for the top in water and smooth it onto the face. Add a bottom piece and then the two strips connecting the top and bottom, down the center of the nose between nostrils. Put the last two pieces on and smooth and mold the lips, eyes, and so on. The quick-drying bandage will set in 2 to 3 minutes. After removing it, paint, and decorate (see page 70).

Caution: Some youngsters are squeamish about having their faces covered. Never force them. Watching the process is also a way to learn.

10

MORE PAPIER-MÂCHÉ

JUST ABOUT ANYTHING

Papier-mâché is very inexpensive and so versatile that you can use it to make just about anything you want. As you have seen, small to large structures can be sculpted using many different supports: modeling clay, rolled newspaper held together with masking tape, balloons, cardboard, stuffed bags.

Small objects can be made in modeling clay with papier-mâché applied directly onto the clay. The object is then cut in half when dry (as for puppet heads—see Chapter 8) and pasted back together again after the clay is removed.

For older children, using flexible wire covered with newspaper for a base for papier-mâché is a fine idea. The wire can be nailed to a wood stand. Human or animal figures can be created and fleshed out with wads of paper. Check out real bodies to see how joints move! Chicken wire is also an excellent material for a base, although care must be taken with the sharp edges. A pair of pliers helps to shape the wire, which can also be nailed with brads, to a plywood stand.

Large to extra-large objects can be made with the stuffed bags. A large shape can be sectioned by tying string tightly around the stuffed item.

PIÑATAS

TIME: Two 30-minute sessions to apply pasted paper, a few days to dry, two 30-minute sessions to decorate

MATERIALS

Sturdy balloons

Papier-mâché paste (see Chapter 8, "Puppets," for alternatives)

Containers for paste and white glue

Newspapers

Cardboard for shapes

Paper towels

Colored tissue

White glue

Water

Scissors

Exacto knife

Small glue brushes

Clothesline

Clothespins

Small groups and some patience will be required for complex constructions. Simplified versions are also possible.

DOING IT Apply papier-mâché as with balloon masks, but cover the whole balloon. Just about any form or character is possible with the addition of cardboard shapes, paper cones, and molded, pasted paper towels. All the shapes of added features should be exaggerated, or they will be lost when covered with tissue. If a shape is long or heavy, cut flanges at the bottom and use tape to secure the flanges to the balloon. A plain globe shape can also be beautiful when decorated.

After three layers of papier-mâché have been applied, hang the piñata by the tied end of the balloon on the clothesline to dry.

When the paste is dry, you or another adult should cut a hole using an Exacto knife, about 4 inches in diameter, for filling the piñata with goodies. Cut only partway around, leaving the piece attached. You will tape the hole shut later. To decorate in the traditional way, cut through several sheets of tissue, making strips 2 to 3 inches wide. Leave five or six strips for streamers, but fringe the rest by cutting into them with parallel cuts, leaving at least ¾ inch uncut so the strip can be glued onto the piñata. Fringed edges can be curled using the edge of the scissors.

To apply the fringe: Thin the white glue by adding an equal amount of water. The colors of wet tissue will run and stain. So before you begin, cover tables with newspaper and have children push up their sleeves. Each child should have enough room around his work space for a pile of fringed tissue on one side and the glue and a brush on the other.

The first step in applying fringe is to draw pencil guidelines to show the placement of the first few rows of tissue. Start at the bottom of the piñata and work outward and upward, overlapping layers. I think the easiest way to attach the fringe is to brush a little glue on the piñata, lay the tissue edge on it, then dab the tissue into place with the glue brush. When fringe is completed, glue on some streamers to fool the would-be piñata bashers.

Younger children can glue on large pieces of tissue or paint their work with tempera and add streamers.

A good group project: several pairs of hands can work together on a piñata—some children can cut the tissue while others paste.

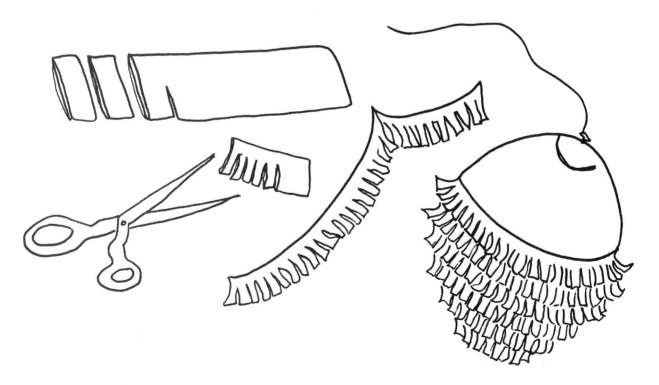

PRINTMAKING

Because printmaking involves so many variables, it gives students as much exposure as possible to this way of working to bring them to an awareness of the special qualities of prints. Children will learn that printmaking is an activity in which persistence pays off. Get tough and don't let them quit until they get a good result—that is, one that they are pleased with. Offer at least two sessions per technique, giving them ample time to explore what does and does not work. This individual learning process can be solidified by an adult-led discussion of students' final prints. Printmaking, in particular, requires this considered approach.

Printing can get messy, so supervision is important. Adults should concentrate on preventing accidents and pointing out materials and how they can be shared. All this needs to be done with sensitivity to the child's thought processes so he or she will not be unduly interrupted. Good work habits can be taught without putting a damper on creativity.

MONOPRINTS

TIME One 15- to 45-minute session for as many children as you have brayers, (two children can share a brayer)

MATERIALS One glass plate per brayer, about 8 by 10 inches, with sharp edges carefully taped

Soft brayers (one to six), rubber tools used for rolling out ink and available at art-supply stores that carry linoleum block–printing materials

Printing inks: A variety of colors

(metallic inks are also available). I use Inko water-soluble inks.

Drawing paper 8½ by 11 inches

Pencils

Popsicle sticks

Clothesline

Clothespins

Optional: Hard brayers

Do some printing on your own so that you will be able to demonstrate this method with confidence.

DOING IT Cover the work area with newspapers. In another area, set up a clothesline for hanging finished prints.

Squeeze ink (about ¾ inch) onto a glass plate. Using a brayer, roll the ink in several directions so it covers the glass with a thin, even coat. Show students that a brayer has a side with a rest so you can set it down without getting ink all over the paper surface.

Children are fascinated by ghost monoprints, which are fainter but often as beautiful as the original design.

Making an inked-line print: Place a sheet of drawing paper lightly on top of the glass. Don't press on it—the ink on the glass will adhere wherever you press. Hold one corner down with a finger so the paper won't slip, then make a drawing on the paper. (You are drawing on the back of the print.) Lift off and voilà! the other side has a nice inked-line print. Children should be warned that they cannot erase lines once they are drawn. For this reason, some may want to make a drawing on scratch paper first. It is best to demonstrate this technique so that they understand the design will be reversed (so all writing must be backwards) and that every little mark and line will become part of the print. By using different strokes to create all sorts of lines, you can introduce the children to the idea of quality of line: soft, harsh, squiggly, bold, and so on. The ink will have to be rolled out again between prints; otherwise, there will be ghost lines in the background. Sometimes these lines turn out to be a happy accident. Older students might utilize this effect in a conscious way. Students can let the first color dry, then add others.

Making a ghostprint: After making your first print, in which the pressure of the pencil point picks up ink for an inked-line print, you can put another paper on the glass and roll a clean brayer or rub with your hand over its surface. The brayer pressure will pick up the ink surrounding the lines (now inkless due to the first print). This will leave a white line with color background printed on your paper.

Alternatively, you may want to draw directly into the ink with a stick. Popsicle sticks turned to utilize both the wide and narrow edges work well. The results of this technique resemble wood-block prints. As in making inked-line prints, you can let the first color dry and add others later.

Printmaking is a repetitive process, and for monoprints that means the first print is often not satisfactory because of too much or not enough ink. Roll it out and try again—it can take some time to achieve the desired plate conditions. You do need to make a new drawing each time—there is no way to save it. (In printing processes capable of producing more than one image, professional artists call their first prints artist's proofs. These are test prints they use to get everything just right.) Children should be strongly encouraged to try making a monoprint several times, until they get something they like. Practice helps, especially when dealing with reversed images.

Hang prints on the clothesline to dry, back to back if necessary.

BLOCK PRINTS

TIME From 15 to 45 minutes

MATERIALS Soft brayers

Printing inks: A variety of colors, water soluble

Pencils with dull points

Styrofoam "blocks" cut from food trays or Plasticine blocks (warm in the sun; press, flatten, and cut it like brownies)

Drawing or construction paper

Optional: Hard brayers

Two children can share a brayer and blocks can be traded.

DOING IT No sharp tools are involved in etching these blocks. A design should be worked out on scratch paper first when using Styrofoam, because once etched, lines cannot be removed.

If your blocks are cut out of food trays, you will want to cut around the maker's stamp pressed in the center. On scratch paper, draw an outline of the piece that will be used as a block, and work a design within its borders.

Use a dull pencil to carve the design into the foam block. Make the lines clear and wide. Styrofoam is not an easy surface to draw on. Straight lines work better than curved ones.

Squeeze ink onto the glass and roll the ink out evenly to coat the brayer. Now roll the inked brayer onto the Styrofoam block until the unmarked surface is covered evenly. You are now ready to print. Take the block and press it facedown on the paper, using a firm hand-on-top-of-hand pressure. Or place the paper on top of the face-up block and roll it with a hard brayer.

After you remove the block, it may or may not need to be inked again before printing. Successive printings in lighter and lighter colors look lovely. The block can also be re-inked with another color. Second, third, or more blocks can be designed and added to the picture.

You can create a continuous design by having the edges match so that, when put together, they make a border or create a larger image.

Blocks of modeling clay (or ceramic clay that is on the dry side) can be carved and printed in much the same way. The blocks should be about 1 inch thick and as large as you can handle. Etch a design, using a dull pencil. As the artist draws in the clay, the displaced clay balls up along the edges of the line. Although this doesn't make any difference with wide, deep lines, it does obscure fine ones. To save the children frustration, warn them that very fine details will probably be lost. The clay can also be pressed with any number of other objects to create textures and patterns. When printing, use a thick pad of newspaper under the paper to be printed. A hard, ungiving surface doesn't work as well with soft blocks.

In block printing, broad, simple, bold designs are best. These are complemented by the appearance of the printed ink, which is often delicate. You can also experiment with printing from blocks of plaster of paris and wax in the same way, using sharper carving tools.

Styrofoam block prints provide subtle color and bold lines.

COLLOGRAPHS

TIME One 30-minute session to make a plate. The glue on the plate should dry overnight. One 15- to 45-minute session to print. Students can bring their own materials to make a plate. Platemaking can be done by a large group all at once, but small groups are recommended for the printing.

MATERIALS Cardboard, such as from cut-up cereal boxes, 7 to 9 inches or larger, one piece per student

White glue in small containers

Brushes for glue

Various materials: Thin sheets of fabric, lace, sandpaper, corrugated paper, string,

feathers, plastic mesh, pipe cleaners, washers, and so on

Tempera paint

Stiff paintbrushes

Paper: Drawing paper sized to fit over 7- by 9-inch cardboard

Optional: Acrylic or polyurethane varnish

DOING IT You can provide all the materials for this project or have the children bring some. They choose the materials they wish to use and arrange them into a design to be glued on to a cardboard backing. Multiple images can be printed from this "plate." To encourage the children to plan their composition, make some samples or have the children make some small test prints. From these, they will get an idea of what the final product will look like.

This project offers a fine opportunity for students to work with the elements of composition without worrying about a theme. They will be moving lines and overlapping planes, creating patterns and juxtaposing textures that will get colored later. Though real or bits of real objects may be used, the result may be totally abstract.

When you are satisfied with the arrangement, outline the items in pencil. The outline will help you reposition the elements after you apply the glue. Remove the pieces one by one, then glue them back into place. Let the glue dry overnight.

At this point, you can coat the plate with an acrylic varnish or polyurethane to hold the materials firmly in place and to provide a harder surface on

which to make your prints. I have never done this extra step and have been satisfied with the results for short runs of five to ten prints.

Before "inking" the plate, the student can make a crayon rubbing on it. This will give him or her an idea of what it will look like. The "ink" (actually tempera paint works fine) is carefully applied with a stiff brush. Several colors can be used as long as one doesn't dry before you finish applying the others. The paint should be brushed on thickly enough to saturate the fibers of the materials, without leaving globs of excess paint, which will spread during the printing process, destroying details of the materials' textures.

Now carefully lay a clean sheet of drawing paper over the plate and rub your hand or roll a brayer over the entire surface. Lift the print and hang it up to dry. If several print are done, they should be numbered. Professional printmakers label the first successful test print "artist's proof," and the subsequent "pulls" are numbered. For an edition of ten prints, the first print after the artist's proof would be 1/10; the second 2/10; and so on. Each print should bear the artist's name and the date of printing in pencil directly under the image.

POTATO PRINTS

TIME One 30-minute session

MATERIALS One half potato per person

Other vegetables: Cabbage,
artichokes, green peppers,
celery bottoms, and so on; citrus
fruit halved the night before
(students can bring these from
home, though you should have a
supply on hand as a backup)

Tempera paint

Flat containers for paint (food
trays work well)

Flat bristle brushes

Knives (dull ones work just fine;
do not have sharp knives loose
in a classroom)

Paper: Butcher paper, drawing
paper, newsprint, tissue paper

Clotheslines

Clothespins

Optional: Set of Japanese
wood-carving tools

It is preferable to have students work in small groups, but it is possible for a large class to work together. Some teachers have desks grouped in fours, facing each other, a setup that would work well for this and other art projects, since students can share colors and tools. One adult per seven students is advised. Three adults could cover a class of thirty at school.

DOING IT Cover work areas with newspapers. Set up a clothesline. Provide an area in which to carve the potatoes (or clear away the carving scraps from the work area before printing). The potatoes can be cut in half lengthwise or cut into halves or into more pieces crosswise. If you can, let each student decide how he or she wants to cut the piece. Ask them to think a little before cutting—to look at the whole shape they have and imagine what shape might be cut out of it. Explain that the uncut parts will be the parts that print. When using dull knives, straight lines are easier to cut than curved ones. For best results, the knife should be angled in for cutting. Make an angled vertical cut and cut in horizontally to remove the part of the potato that will be outside the design. You can work

Anne-Rachelle Trimble uses several designs she carved by herself as well as some she traded with friends.

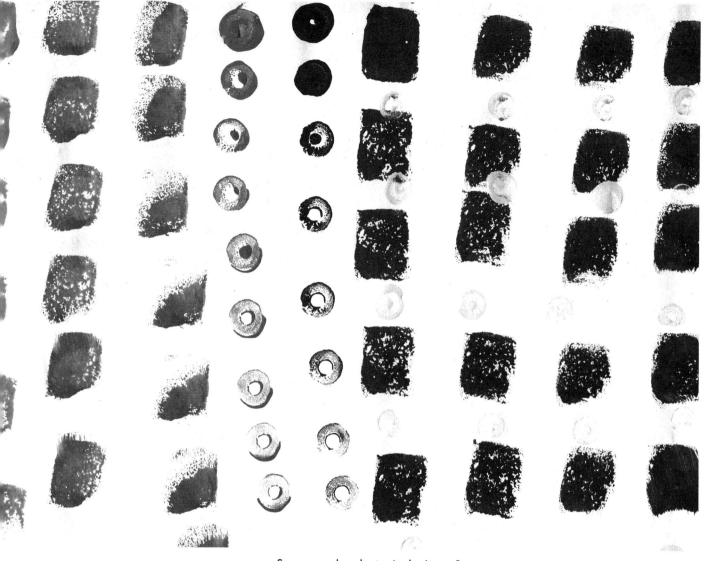

Sponge and gadget print by Isaac Sever

within the rounded edge of the potato or trim it away to create your own shape. Start with a simple shape like a triangle and see how it can be combined to make more complex shapes. Try a shape with more than one element—for instance, stripes. Try a continuous design with carvings that have matching edges.

Some children will carve and carve until only a nub is left. Before giving them another potato, I ask them to picture what they want to carve. If they can't, I make simple suggestions, but it is better to let them watch what others are doing or to have them work with something like a square printed in several colors, layers, and patterns.

After the carving is done, put out a wide selection of tempera colors in flat containers or plates. Most young children, and many older ones, will use only the colors near them. Encourage them to move around the work space or to trade to get colors not immediately near them.

Potatoes can be dipped in the paint (though this is messy) or color can be painted on with brushes. Children may get carried away with stamping, since they don't have to re-ink between each stamp. The resulting gradations of color can be quite beautiful. Encourage trading and recarving or new carving. Potato prints can be complete compositions on their own or used to make cards or wrapping paper. They can also be used on fabric with fabric paint.

If the students use vegetables in addition to potatoes, notice the variety of patterns in the leaves and seeds.

SPONGE PRINTS

TIME One 30-minute session. Plan on a little more cleanup time to include washing the sponges and other objects.

MATERIALS Newspapers

Clothesline

Clothespins

Sponges: Have a few basic shapes precut and enough bigger pieces for students to cut at least one of their own. The foam that comes as packing material is wonderful for making prints. It is about ½ inch thick and is easy to cut.

Other objects: Spools, brushes, bolts, and all manner of hardware, kitchen utensils, rubber alphabet sets, and whatever you can hold in your hand and apply paint to

Tempera paint

Flat containers for paint and for holding painted objects

Assorted paintbrushes

Assorted paper: Construction, drawing, tissue, and so on

DOING IT Cover work areas with newspapers. Set up a clothesline. Set out a good assortment of objects and of paints within easy reach of each child. Empty trays for paint-covered objects are also useful. If paint does get spilled on the work area, put down a new sheet of newspaper for the next person. Once again, point out all the colors and objects and encourage the children to try also using materials other than what is immediately handy.

Once the students have had plenty of opportunity to print freely, offer them a specific project. For example, fold a piece of paper in half, in half again, and so on, until a grid of boxes, each measuring 3 to 4 inches, is formed. Students can then print within these grids, using a variety of objects. Make sure that there are a wide variety of shapes—small and large, open and closed forms—and a variety of textures in order to create a visual balance. This project need not become "Lesson No. 4: Balance." It's just one of the many ways to heighten visual awareness by doing, noticing, and storing visual memories.

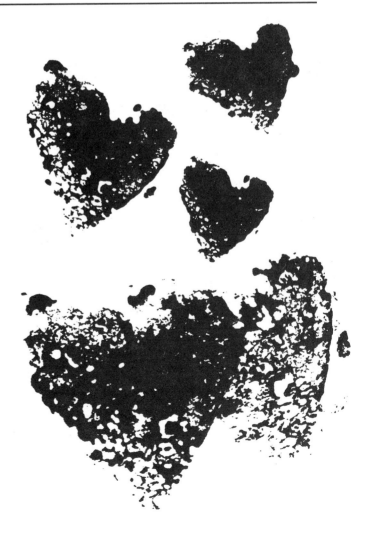

Rachel Sever figured out how to combine one design with itself by matching edges for a continuous print (at the age of six).

SCREEN PRINTS

Silkscreen printing requires some professional equipment for the long term, but you can make a cardboard-framed temporary screen for children to try out this technique without going to great expense. There is also a plastic frame now available to use with thermal stencils, as discussed in this chapter (page 85). Because silkscreening is complicated, I recommend that before using a screen children work with stencils in a more direct way by cutting out shapes from tracing paper and painting or coloring in cutout areas. This will give them an understanding of what designs work well in stencils. Most of the stencil types used in making professional screen prints are not appropriate for projects with children. This chapter includes two that are appropriate for children to use.

TRACING PAPER STENCILS

TIME If using homemade screens, you will need to make cardboard-framed screens ahead of time for younger children. Allow 30 minutes to an hour for yourself or older children to make screens. Unless everyone has his or her own screen, children will be sharing, so it is best to have the group pick one design to print. If it's a small group, stencils can be changed several times. Allow two 30-minute sessions for a simple project. Allow one session for designing and cutting the stencil and one for printing.

MATERIALS Screen: If you plan on doing a fair amount of printing, you may want to invest in a store-bought screen. A screen is a wooden frame with a synthetic fabric (silk is hardly used anymore) stretched and stapled or held in grooves around the frame. Ready-made screens are available at art-supply stores. Or, make a cardboard frame.

Squeegee: A rubber or nylon strip mounted on a handle. The strip should fit inside the screen. Heavy cardboard can be used for short print runs.

Tracing paper

Layout paper (plain white stock) somewhat larger than the image area of the screen

Scratch paper

Tempera paint

Spatula, for scraping paint from screen

Spoon

Scissors

Clothesline

Clothespins

Rulers

Pencils

Masking tape

Optional: Heavy cardboard, cotton organdy or lightweight cotton fabric, mat knife or Exacto knife

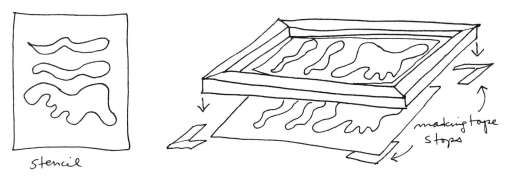

stencil

masking tape stops

DOING IT

Making a cardboard screen: Draw a square or rectangle inside a piece of heavy cardboard, leaving enough border for strength. Cut out this piece using a mat knife. Tape all four edges of a piece of cotton fabric to the back of the cardboard so that it covers the opening, making the fabric as tight as you can. The cardboard screen will not hold up for any length of time but will demonstrate the process very well. You can use a strip of cardboard as a squeegee.

Making the stencil: As with most printing processes, one color is laid down at a time. Stick with one-color designs until students see how the process works.

Printing in one color: You need a large, smooth-surfaced work table. If your screen is not too big, laminated sink cutouts make great portable printing surfaces. A wooden screen can be attached to the cutout with removable pin hinges. It is essential that the screen and paper be returned to a fixed position between each printing.

Cut the layout paper to be compatible with the size of your screen. Before cutting the stencil, try out some designs on scratch paper of the same size. Remember that the design will be made into a stencil and must be all of a piece. When you have an image with which you are satisfied, finalize the design on layout paper. First, draw a frame large enough to encompass the image, making sure it is centered on the layout paper. Now draw the image inside the frame (it should touch the edges at the widest and highest points). Trace the design with tracing paper. The tracing paper should be centered over the design and should have a wide border area. This paper will become the stencil when you have cut out the areas to be printed with color.

You will use the layout paper to align your design on the screen. Lay the paper down on the table or Formica cutout and mark with masking tape the upper-right and lower-left corners. Use several pieces of tape, one on top of the other, so papers can be slipped in and held in place. Leaving your layout paper in place within its stops, place your stencil over the layout paper. Carefully lower the screen. If it is not fixed with pin hinges, be sure to mark its position with tape on the table in upper-left and lower-right corners so that it will be returned to the same position relative to the paper.

Place three or four spoonfuls of tempera paint near the top of the screen. When printing with small children, an adult should stand on the other side of the table and hold down the screen if it is not hinged to the surface. Children can take the squeegee and pull it toward themselves, using both hands and holding the squeegee at an angle, all the way past the bottom of the stencil. A steady, even pressure is what you want. The paint will make the stencil stick to the screen. Push the paint back to the top of the screen in the same way. Clean, dry fabric may take more than two passes to get saturated. Set the squeegee on a can or box so that it doesn't get paint all over the table. Lift the screen: The stencil will have blocked the paint while the fabric let it through. Hang the print on the clothesline to dry.

Printing in more than one color: The trick to printing additional colors is getting them to land in the right spot (to be in registration). Once you've printed one time, you can't see through the screen anymore. To do two colors, print your first color and put your second stencil on top of the printed color. Where colors meet, they should overlap a bit. Registration with tracing-paper stencils will be tricky because they tend to move around when you lower the screen. The design should be made with this in mind—don't worry about precision and allow for some slight movement. A bit of white edge between can even add to the visual interest. Experience will show you how to plan for such variations.

THERMAL SCREENS

TIME Two 30-minute sessions, one for design and one for printing. If appropriate, children can come to print one at a time, in a corner of a busy classroom, with one adult to oversee printing and another person designated to hang the prints.

MATERIALS Thermofax machine (public schools have them)

Copy machine

Thermal screens: These special screens, along with plastic frames, are available in thermal printing kits that include squeegee and water-soluble fabric inks. Welsh Products (PO Box 845, Benecia, CA 94510; 707-745-3252) carries a "Tryout Kit" with 4 screens, an economical way for a small or large group to get started. It also contains inks, frames, and a squeegee. A large group may use only one stencil if doing a project like a class T-shirt.

Squeegee

Scratch paper

Pencils

Tempera paint or water-soluble inks for paper and fabric

Spatula

Spoon

Clothesline

Clothespins

Objects to be printed: Paper, fabric, or T-shirts

Newspapers (if printing T-shirts)

Before participating in a thermal-printing project, I highly recommend that children work with other, less technical kinds of stencils, so that they will understand how this technique works. Otherwise, it will be merely one more mysterious process.

DOING IT After determining the final size of your print, work out possible designs on scratch paper. Draw the final design using a medium that can be copied clearly on a copy machine.

The beauty of this process is that a child's drawing can be exactly reproduced in all its spontaneity. If you are working with a large group, children can vote on a design for a group project—for example, a class T-shirt. The design could consist of an arrangement of the drawings of several people.

Thermal screens come with complete instructions. Essentially, thermal-screen printing is a process of copying the final design and passing that copy through a thermofax machine on top of a thermal screen. The screen will melt away where the dark lines of the drawing are and leave an open mesh to print through. Printing proceeds in the same manner as for silk screens. T-shirts should always have a double thickness of newspaper slipped between front and back to prevent ink from seeping through. Thermal screens have greatly simplified group T-shirt projects and allowed reproduction of actual children's art (although children are not in on the stencil-making process).

To learn more about the qualities of good printmaking, see the works of Rembrandt, the Japanese master Kawasé Hirosage, Raoul Dufy, Jim Dine, Sister Mary Corita, and Andy Warhol.

12

FABRIC

SEWING WITH CHILDREN

HAND-SEWING WITH A GROUP

Everyone can sew. Many children seem to know how to sew by hand, but there are some who have never sewed or are reluctant. I get everybody hand-sewing; even if we are machine-sewing, there are always parts that must be done by hand. It is a good idea to have several needles threaded before beginning. I always double the thread so it doesn't slip out of the needle. Also, be aware that children often leave too little thread at the end of a row to make a knot. I ask them to stop with about 4 inches of thread left so that I can show them how to make a knot.

MACHINE-SEWING WITH CHILDREN SIX AND UP

Use a sturdy machine with a straight needle (I would not use a slant needle with children). Briefly explain the basic parts of the machine and show them how to work the foot. Help guide the fabric with your left hand, being careful not to obstruct the child's view. The child should hold the fabric loosely with his or her left hand at the top, *away from the needle,* and the right hand down at the bottom of the fabric. Use a foot pedal (making sure that it is within comfortable reach) and have the child keep his or her heel on the floor for better control.

When the child is comfortable in this position, have him or her make a couple of practice rows on a scrap. Then go right ahead and seam up a pillow or a puppet costume. These simple projects are fun

Sewing is a favorite with children. Newly acquired skills quickly get put to use when a child is inspired by projects like creating wind socks (above).

and well within the expertise of first-time sewers.

Sometimes an adult will take over and do the sewing for the children, producing exciting, elaborate costumes—but the child is not participating. Learning to sew by machine is an excellent opportunity for children to work one-on-one with an adult to learn how to safely use a machine. Doing the sewing for them precludes this exploration.

When sewing in a large classroom, there should always be an extra adult to supervise; a full-time person is needed at the machine. I love this time to work closely with individual children and see them go from being unsure of their ability to beaming over the final product.

NOT JUST ANY OLD PILLOWS

TIME About 30 minutes total to complete a pillow, depending on adult help at the sewing machine

MATERIALS Fabric scraps (These are easy to acquire, just ask and they will rain in on you; be sure to ask that they are no smaller than 12 inches square.)

Scissors: Use good-quality ones for fabric, or children will not be able to cut their own. (There are excellent small scissors available with bright plastic handles.) Have *at least* one pair and several others of average quality for cutting thread.

Paper

Pencils

Masking tape

Thread (also easy to acquire through donations)

Needles and pins (pincushions expedite work)

Fabric crayons (I use Pentel)

Fiberfill

Sewing machine

Iron

Optional: Batting (for quilted pillows)

DOING IT To create a personally designed pillow, the child should decide its size and shape. He or she should then make a paper pattern to represent this design and use it to cut out two pieces of solid fabric. Have the children draw a few practice designs on the pattern itself or on a paper of the same size. Make sure to leave room for seam allowances around the edges. When you complete a design that you like, copy it in fabric crayon on the solid fabric piece. Fabric crayon doesn't erase, so the preliminary drawing is important. Tape the fabric to a smooth tabletop so it doesn't slip around.

Using an iron, heat-set the crayon drawing according to instructions on the crayon package. Children love to iron, and I generally let them do it while standing very nearby. After the drawing is set, sew up the pillow's seams, leaving an opening for stuffing. Clip the seam allowance diagonally at the corners for the children, very close to the stitching. They will see how this makes a pointed corner when the pillowcase is turned right side out. Have the child turn the pillow right side out, then stuff it. Help the child to hand-sew the opening.

Older students can make quilted pillows by adding a layer of batting behind the design and quilting around the design elements by machine or hand.

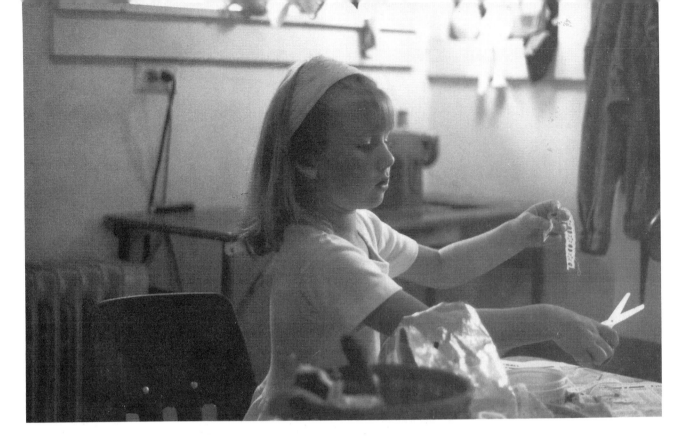

WALL HANGINGS AND ASSORTED PROJECTS

TIME From 15 minutes to several hours

MATERIALS Materials needed vary by project.

DOING IT Fabric pictures can be made to hang on the walls for special occasions or for everyday. Fabric crayons, paint, and patchwork appliquéd with or without batting can be used. Stitching produced by the sewing machine can be used to "draw" details. Fabric pictures can even be made into simple window shades by running a dowel through the top and bottom to hang on hooks on either side of the window. Simple flat purses, bookbags, flags, and banners are other possibilities that are popular.

Some children have even made wonderful dolls. Sock dolls are a great way to start. The end of the sock is stuffed and tied off to create a head. The bottom ribbed part is cut in half to form legs. The same area is cut off another sock to make arms. This is an especially good beginning project as the stretchy fabric is easy to sew when stuffed. Sock dolls do not have to be human. For a good selection of pattern ideas, see *Rags* by Linda and Stella Alli-

son. Dolls such as the one pictured on page 90 (upper left) require much more planning and pattern making, but if the desire and determination are there, results can be outstanding. For beginners, sock puppets may be a solution; just sew on some button eyes and maybe a tongue or tuft of fur and the children have transformed an object into art.

The sewing cabinet in my classroom contains as many fabric swatches as possible as well as other donated materials: leather and vinyl scraps, beads, jewelry, shells, elastic, decorative seam tapes and rickrack, laces, velvet, felt scraps, old crochet pieces, and more. Sometimes these materials inspire a unique creation that we never would have thought of, such as the leather hat and shield resembling a Native American ritual costume put together by one young man. The doors to the cabinet are open and children are free to poke through its contents. Whenever possible, we like to keep our doors open. Art making is also about trust.

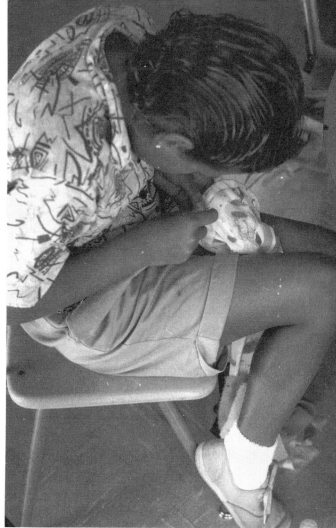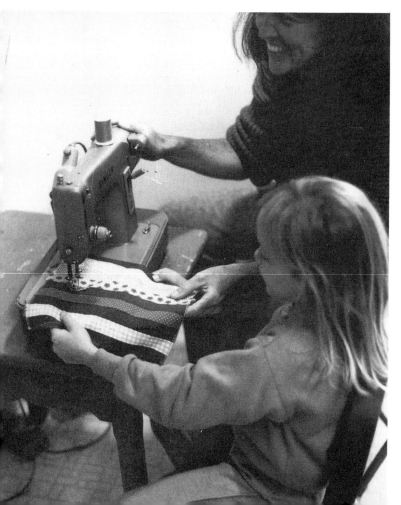

WIND SOCKS

TIME Two sessions: about 20 minutes for painting design (paint must dry overnight) and 30 minutes for sewing

MATERIALS Fabric: Make sure to have some plain white fabric such as cut-up sheets or new cotton or cotton blends cut into rectangles at least 12 by 18 inches (they can be larger)

Ribbons, seam bindings, or filmy fabric cut in 18-inch strips

Fabric paint: I dilute acrylic paint with water and have found that it holds up well outdoors

Soft paintbrushes (I use Japanese brush-painting brushes)

Jars for paint

Newspapers

Heavy plain paper or cardboard

Coat hangers (you can get them free from the dry cleaners)

Wire cutters

Pliers

Scissors

Pins

Needles

Sewing machine

Heavy yarn

Optional: One-pound coffee can

DOING IT

Preparing for the project: If you are working with a large group, you may want to precut and bend the coat-hanger wire into circles for the tops of the wind socks. Cut wire into lengths to fit the desired width of the socks. A 1-pound coffee can makes a good form to bend the wire around (it is about the same diameter as a 12-inch-wide sock), but you can do just as well with your hands and pliers. Older children can do this for themselves. If using acrylic paint, thin it by adding a small amount of water a little at a time until it reaches a consistency that enables you to paint it onto fabric using a soft-bristled brush. The paint should not be so thin that the color is diluted.

Making the wind socks: Cover a table with newspapers and set out a complete selection of paint colors and brushes. The fabric to be painted should be on top of a heavy piece of plain paper or board. After painting, the material must sit overnight to dry. When dry, lay the fabric out and arrange ribbon streamers along the bottom of the sock on the wrong side. Pin the streamers to the sock, then machine- or hand-sew them. Seam the wind sock, but leave it wrong side out. Fit a wire circle to the top of the sock, fold ⅝ inch of fabric over the wire, and pin the folded fabric. Use an overcast stitch to create a hem with the wire inside. Turn the stock right side out and add heavy yarn at the top to serve as a hanger.

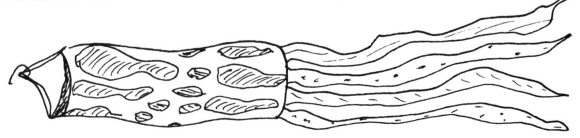

13

YARN

DROP-SPINDLE SPINNING

TIME Flexible: At least 15 minutes to get going, the first time, and then for however long you want. Students will need at least 5 minutes of one-on-one instruction to start and a few more to keep going.

MATERIALS Drop spindles: Easy to make yourself by using potatoes or apples with a stick stuck through each. For more permanent spindles, Janet Jenkins and I made whorls of clay with shafts of ⅝-inch dowel.

Knitting yarn (to serve as starter thread)

Fleece: Should be hand-spinning quality. Long-fibered fleece (or staple) makes spinning easier for children. Check the spinning and weaving periodicals at the library, which often offer fleece for sale. Feed stores are another source of information.

Penknife

Once you become aware that it is possible to spin without a spinning wheel, new horizons open. I'm including an outline of the basics, but spinning is something that you should learn by working with an experienced person. These instructions can be used as a memory aid in case your expert isn't available and you just gotta spin.

DOING IT

Making shafts: Cut the ⅝-inch dowel into 7-inch lengths. With a penknife, make a *V*-shaped cut, or notch, in the top of the dowel to hold the strands of wool as you spin. Score around the dowel 1 inch from the bottom. To taper the shaft and leave a little seat for the whorl to rest on snugly, shave the shaft from partway down to the score line.

Making whorls: Make clay disks about 2¼ inches in diameter and ¾ inch thick. With one of the dowel shafts, poke a hole through the center of each. Bisque-fire the clay.

Spinning:

1. Tie a starter thread (a piece of knitting yarn) to the drop spindle below the whorl.

2. Bring the thread over the whorl. Wrap the thread around the shaft, above the whorl, crossing the thread over itself and then bringing it up to the notch at the top of the shaft.

3. Make a simple half hitch around the notch.

4. Holding the ball of fleece (unspun wool) with your right hand, overlap it onto the starter thread, so the fleece and thread will twist together. Turn the spindle with your left hand in a clockwise direction until you feel the spin tighten in the fingers of your right hand.

5. Place the spindle between your knees or feet (depending on the length of the yarn). Switch hands without letting go of the yarn. With your left hand holding the top of the tightly spun yarn, draw out the fleece with your right hand and then let go with the left hand; watch the spin travel up to your right hand. The spin will go up as far as you drew it out. Repeat until you've run out of spinning fleece.

6. Repeat spinning and drawing out the wool until the yarn is so long that it must be rolled onto the shaft. Wind it on the shaft, above the whorl. Wind more yarn at the bottom of the shaft, then toward the top.

7. When the shaft is full of spun yarn, wind it on someone's hands or on the back of a chair to make a skein. If you want to wash the yarn, tie the skein in several places with loose figure-eight ties to hold the yarn in place. Twist the skein into a coil.

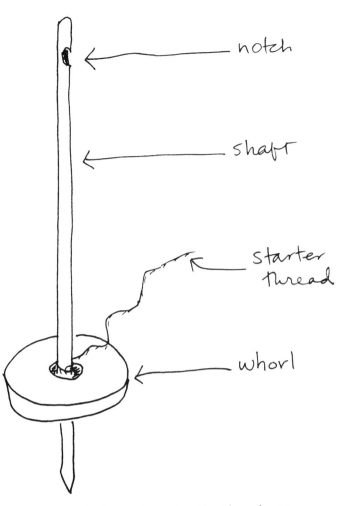

Above: Drop spindles can be made with sticks and potatoes, apples, or homemade clay whorls. If possible, give children the opportunity to try spinning with a wheel (below). Spinners can use their own homespun yarn for weaving pockets (below left).

POCKET WEAVING

TIME **Preparing to weave:** Allow an hour or two to make several looms.
Weaving: This project can take from 1 to 4 hours, depending on the student. I let students take their little looms home with enough yarn to weave a bit, although I ask them to use their own needles. Some parents have told me about their children working nonstop at home or on long car trips. Plan on 5 minutes of one-on-one to get the weavings started. Then an adult will need to check in every once in a while to see if things are proceeding smoothly.

MATERIALS Cardboard rectangles, 4 by 6 inches

Rulers

Pencils

String

Yarn: A wide selection of colors

and weights (short lengths are okay and will add color variety)

Large-eyed, blunt needles

Pick comb(s)

Optional: Little beads, shells, feathers, charms

Although there are several ways to weave without a regular loom that are well documented in books on weaving, I include only one here. This project is suitable for most children over seven and creates a beautiful and useful product.

DOING IT

Creating the looms: Cut a cardboard rectangle for each child. Using a ruler, mark off an evenly spaced series of dots about ⅜ inch apart and about ½ inch from the top of the cardboard. Punch a hole in each dot with a large, sharp needle. Thread a needle with string and sew in and out of the holes, front and back, filling in all the spaces between them. Tie off the string. Then thread a needle with yarn, choosing a color to be the warp thread (which runs lengthwise in the weaving).

Warping the loom: Older children can warp their own looms; you will have to do this for younger children. Notch the end of the cardboard loom, at the top, with a ¼-inch slit near one edge. Knot the end of your yarn and slip it in the notch. Run the yarn down and around, under the bottom of the cardboard and up the other side; through the first string stitch; and back down and around and up through the first stitch on the other side of the loom. Con-

tinue until you have gone through all the string stitches on both sides of the loom, adding one extra row. You should have an odd number of rows. Tie the yarn at the bottom. The loom is now completely warped.

Weaving: Have the children choose their first piece of yarn. This color will be at the top of the weaving. Thread the needle with the chosen yarn. Threading yarn is easier if you wet the end, bend ½ inch of it around the needle, and pull it up sharply to crease it. Push the creased end through the eye. Now students can begin to weave their pocket, going over and under the warp threads. When they get to the end of a row, they continue on around the back, and around and around, to make what will be a tubular weaving. Lengths of yarn shouldn't exceed a yard; they can be shorter. The student can change colors as often as he or she likes by tying yarns together. Changing textures and weights is interesting and little beads or charms can also be woven into the outside.

After doing three or four rows, use the pick comb to push the rows of weaving close together toward the top of the loom. As children go along, make sure that if one row goes over under, over under, the next row goes under over, under over.

When the children get down to the bottom, have them try to squeeze as many rows in as possible, stitching in and out of each individual warp one at a time. Tie off the end. Now snip the string stitches at the top and slip the pocket off the loom.

Varying the weave: For a twill pattern, make sure to have an odd number of warp threads. Go over and under two at a time.

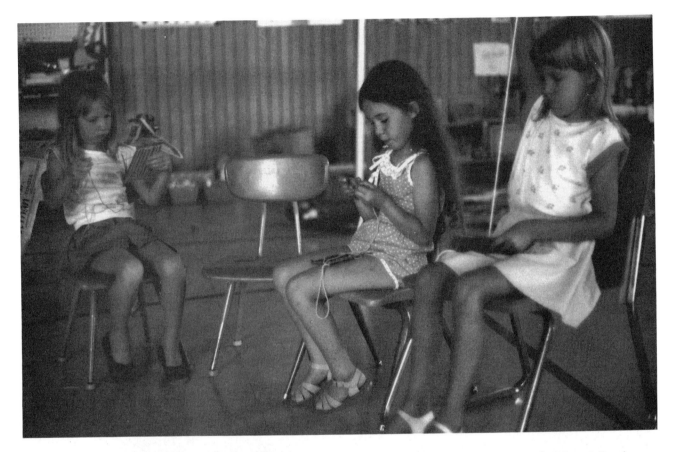

A trio of pocket weavers works intently (above). Teacher Janet Jenkins helps a student start a drop spindle (left). Pockets can be of as many different colors as the weaver chooses and provide hours of fun (below).

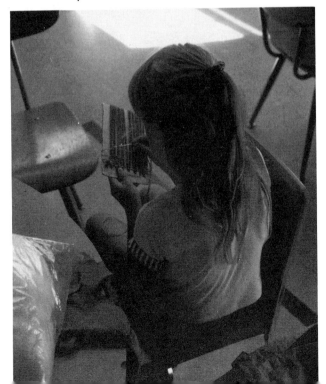

TWISTED CORD

TIME About 15 minutes

MATERIALS Yarn

Scissors

Doorknob (attached to a door!)

This wonderful and simple craft is learned at school by every Swiss child.

DOING IT Cut a length of yarn four times as long as you want the finished cord to be. Fold it in half and tie the ends together. Put scissors through the loop at the knotted end. Loop the other end over a doorknob. Step back until the yarn is straight and taut. Turn the scissors to turn the yarn, holding it taut. Twist until it's even looking and fairly tight. Test it by releasing tension. If it starts to twist upon itself, it's ready.

Put scissors down on the ground with a heavy book on top to hold them in place while you cut the other end of the yarn off the doorknob. Hold the ends tightly together, bring them back to the scissors, and tie them together on the scissors. If the yarn starts to twist now, gently pull it straight. Pick up the middle of the yarn, and drop the scissors and watch them spin while the cord twists on itself from bottom to top. Stop when the twist reaches the top. Cut off the scissors and knot the ends of the yarn.

These cords make a nice drawstring to turn a pocket weaving into a pouch.

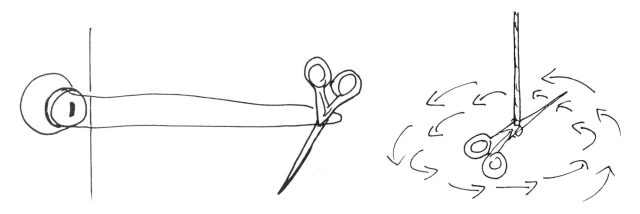

GOD'S EYE

TIME About 30 minutes. Plan on a few minutes one-on-one with each child; children can also teach each other.

MATERIALS Yarn: Varied colors and weights (short lengths are okay)

Sticks: Natural sticks are nicest but any sticks, even Popsicle sticks, will work. (I collect sticks from our neighborhood eucalyptus after a storm—they smell good!)

Scissors

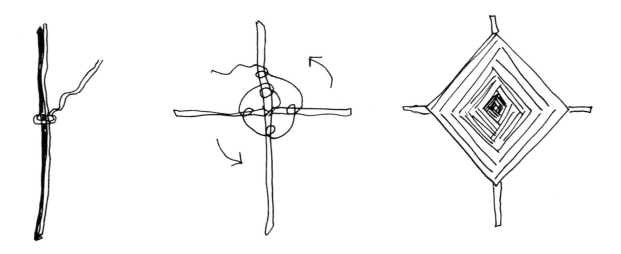

A Mexican tradition, a god's eye is made when a baby is born to ward off evil spirits. One of young people's favorite projects, these are excellent for improving the muscle skills needed for reading by training the eye to track.

DOING IT Choose two sticks and cut about a yard of a starting yarn color. Hold the sticks side by side and tie them firmly around the center, knotting them together. Twist them open into a cross shape.

Wrap yarn around and under each stick, turning as you go. Children can chant to themselves "Un-der, around, and turn; under, around, and turn." Change colors as often as you like by knotting the old color to the new. When done, the loose ends are pushed through the back of the god's eye.

The traditional god's eye combines warm and cool colors with warm at the center. It's nice to have a traditional one on hand, but encourage creativity. If you are using long sticks, you can make small god's eyes at the end of each one to complement the center. Tiny god's eyes on tooth picks can be used as holiday ornaments, on a Christmas tree, for example.

YARN PAINTING

TIME Two or more 30-minute sessions

MATERIALS Yarn: Should be soft, smooth, and of similar weight. Thick rug yarn will be easier for young children to handle. Very bright colors are traditional.

White glue
Containers for glue
Brushes for glue
Cardboard backings

This is an adaptation of the art of the Huichol Indians of northern Mexico. Their paintings have evolved from a very old form of offering, or *nierika*, which represented requests to the gods by means of yarn designs pressed into beeswax on wood squares or circles.

DOING IT Most Huichols do not make a preliminary sketch but work directly on the wax. This project can be approached in that way to achieve greater spontaneity.

Make a sample yourself, and share a book on actual Huichol paintings with your students. They

will need to know for what they're aiming.

Brush glue on small areas of the cardboard at a time. It's best to work from the center out so you aren't resting your hand on a part that's just been done. Start in the center of a design element and wrap yarn around or back and forth, leaving no space in between strands for the cardboard to show through. All kinds of shapes can be formed—it is also fine to simply work without a plan. Each work table or desk should have a wide selection of yarn colors. With a large group, it is helpful to precut yarn lengths. This will encourage children to use different colors and lengths of yarn and will facilitate sharing.

Very bright, high-contrast colors are traditional. Outlining shapes with a contrasting color is also common. Children should be informed about the traditional style of the craft, and also be allowed to invent their own variations.

Owl yarn painting and artist Alicia Boudreaux (left)

BASKETMAKING

SIMPLE COIL BASKET

TIME From 1 to 2 hours, broken up into smaller periods. Each child will need several minutes of one-on-one instruction.

MATERIALS Clothesline: Natural fiber for basket core, about 1 yard per person

Raffia or yarn for weft

Blunt-end tapestry or darning needles

Scissors

Optional: Little beads or shells

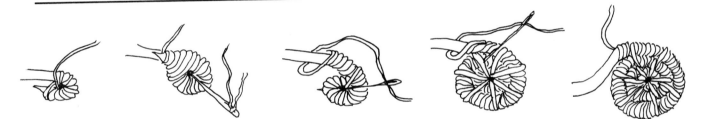

There are detailed books available on basket weaving. The following is one of the simpler and more successful projects.

DOING IT To make this basket, you will use the Lazy Squaw stitch (see above). Trim the end of the core material on a slant. Thread a yard of raffia or yarn through a needle. Hold end of raffia and tapered end of core together with one hand and wrap raffia twice over core for about 2 inches. Holding raffia in place, bend the core into as tight a loop as you can. Tuck rough end of core under.

Hold loop and wrap raffia tightly over joining until secured. Put needle down through the center.

Wind the raffia, front to back, around the core four times. Wrap raffia over core and into the center of the coil circle. Pull tightly and hold. Wrap raffia around the core again four times and bring it through the center again. Continue, always wrapping tightly, until two coils are completed.

For a perfectly round basket, you'll need to mark the beginning of each row with a marker thread. Continue to wrap four times and drop the needle down two coiled rows, always inserting the needle into the front so you can see what you're doing. As you increase the rows and the coil grows larger, increase the number of wraps as needed. You can then shape the coils into a basket form as you go. A few children leave theirs flat.

Shells and beads can be threaded on the weft and incorporated into these baskets.

To make the basket bigger, cut the ends of the old and the new core pieces so that they taper. Join them, making sure they overlap at least 2 inches.

To end the basket, taper the end of the core material and wrap it tightly with weft until secure.

MODELING DOUGHS

Salt-and-cornstarch dough can also be worked similarly to baker's clay. Although it has a different texture and may not be quite as flexible, salt-and-cornstarch dough doesn't need to be baked. Children can put their work on a Styrofoam tray to take home. (Make sure names are on trays!)

BAKER'S CLAY

TIME About 30 minutes to mix and color dough and 30 minutes or more to make things

MATERIALS Baker's clay (see the recipe that follows to determine amounts of flour, salt, and water)

Heavy paper or cardboard

Aluminum foil

Cookie sheets

Powdered tempera or food coloring

Paper clips

Objects to press into dough:

Assorted knives, toothpicks, nails, etc.

Mixing bowls

Measuring cups

Mixing spoons

Garlic press

Polyurethane

A large group can work together with one or two adults. It is best to use dough the same day, but it can be stored overnight if wrapped in plastic and kept in a cool place.

DOING IT

Mixing and coloring the dough: If the group is large, this should be done ahead of time. The following ingredients provide enough dough for six people:

4 cups flour
1 cup salt
1½ cups water

To prepare white dough, in a large mixing bowl mix flour and salt. Stir in the water, then knead the dough until it is soft.

To prepare colored dough, begin by choosing whether to use tempera or food coloring. Tempera makes opaque colors. Food coloring makes translu-

Modeling-dough art is an ideal project for doing at home. Everything you need is probably right there in your kitchen.

tached, or the features may fall off when the piece dries). Toothpicks can be used to make details; any number of objects or textures can be pressed in. Large balls can be flattened into plaque shapes with a hole at the top for hanging. Small objects not affected by the heat of the oven, like seeds or beans, can also be incorporated. Give each child a piece of aluminum foil on which to put their finished piece, and have them stick a paper clip carefully into its top, to serve as a hanger.

Baking and coating the dough: Unbaked dough can air-dry until firm enough to be taken home to bake. Place dough onto a foil-covered cookie sheet for baking. Uncolored dough can be baked at 325° Fahrenheit for about 2 hours or until hard. Colored dough should be baked at a lower temperature, 200° to 225° Fahrenheit, for 3 to 4 hours. A coating of polyurethane after baking will preserve and brighten colors.

cent colors. If using tempera, add the powder to the dry ingredients. If using food coloring, add the color to the water. You can divide the recipe into four smaller batches, adding color to three parts and leaving one white as you like. Or, you can make four full batches for a large group, coloring three of them. Additional colors can be created by kneading colored doughs together, or adding food coloring directly to small bits of dough for lots of choices. Make a well in the dough and drip in a few drops of coloring at a time. Knead until blended. This can be messy, and food coloring stains, so take precautions. See color mixing instructions on package and in the painting chapter.

Modeling the dough: Balls and snakes are the basic building shapes. Balls should not be more than 1 inch in diameter or they will take forever to bake and may crack. Give each child a piece of heavy paper or cardboard to work on, and make sure everyone has access to all the colors and tools by placing them in the center.

Baker's clay is extremely versatile. It can be twisted and braided and run through a garlic press. Tiny, tiny features can be rolled between the fingers and stuck on (make sure they are securely at-

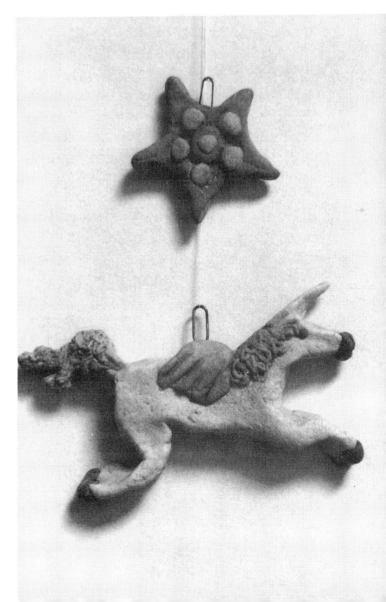

SALT-AND-CORNSTARCH DOUGH

TIME About 35 minutes to prepare, 30 to 60 minutes to make things.

MATERIALS Salt-and-cornstarch dough (see the recipe that follows to determine amounts of salt, cornstarch, and water)

Double boiler

Wooden spoon

Food coloring

Cardboard

Modeling tools

Paper clips

Garlic press

Mixing bowls

Measuring cups

Plastic wrap

Styrofoam food trays

Large groups can work together. Dough must be used the same day it is cooked.

DOING IT

Mixing the dough: The following ingredients provide enough dough for three people:

> 1 cup salt
> ½ cup cornstarch
> ¾ cup water

In the top of the double boiler, mix salt and cornstarch. Add the water and use the wooden spoon to stir well, until ingredients are dissolved. Over low to medium heat, stir constantly for a few minutes, until the mixture gets rubbery and hard to stir. When it starts to pull away from the sides of the pot (not long after it thickens), it is done. Turn out the dough and let it cool until just warm to the touch. Then shape it into a ball. Keep the dough wrapped in plastic wrap until ready to use.

To color, make smaller balls, punch a well with your thumb in the center of each, drop in food coloring, and knead the dough. Do this on a piece of cardboard—the coloring will stain. Large amounts of color can be made by adding food coloring to water before mixing. Try at least one tablespoon of coloring per batch but do save some uncolored dough.

16

WOOD

TIME At least 30 minutes. In fact, as long as you want! This activity seems to have limitless appeal.

MATERIALS Smooth, precut wood scraps (I get mine from a local cabinet shop); sort the wood into small, medium, and large sizes.

Wood glue

Containers for glue

Brushes for glue

Masking tape

Paint

Paintbrushes

Things to add to the wood:

Wallpaper, upholstery, and rug samples; tile samples; fabric; plastic caps; newspapers; metal lids; modeling wax; etc.

In my classes we approach work with wood as art rather than carpentry. We don't use saws, hammers, or nails. Because we collect a great variety of sizes and shapes of wood, there isn't really any need to cut size.

DOING IT Cover tables with newspaper. Since we use glue and no nails, it's a good idea to find a large piece of wood to serve as a base. Glue should be liberally brushed on the edges of both pieces to be glued together. Some children know exactly how to make this work; others will need help getting the glued pieces to stay in place. After gluing a piece at a right angle to the base, glue a narrow strip of wood along the inside seam (to provide support). Masking tape can hold the pieces in place until dry.

We allow the students free rein and watch for those who become frustrated and start to give up. Some of the constructions in wood are abstract—collages of wood. Others are real things: ships, trees, people, guitars, shelves, cars, and, most of all, houses.

Providing hours of fun, wood-scrap houses can be filled with handmade furnishings, such as this one by Angela Eberle.

CARDBOARD

CYLINDER CITIES: A GROUP PROJECT

TIME Two to four 30-minute periods of reading and discussion, four to six 40-minute periods for making cities

MATERIALS One large cardboard base per group (a side of a refrigerator carton is perfect); a large selection of cardboard cylinders: rolls for toilet paper, paper towels, wrapping paper, and carpeting; oatmeal and salt boxes and so on

White glue

Scissors

Exacto knife, for use by an adult

Tempera paints

Paintbrushes

Containers for paint

Optional: A selection of plastic or metal lids and similar objects

Students work in groups of six or seven. A large group can be supervised by one teacher and an aide.

DOING IT

Preparing for the project: This group project needs to be planned in advance. It works better in the second half of the school year, when students know each other. Also, cylinders can be collected during winter break, when those nice, big wrapping-paper tubes become available.

Prepare the group for a discussion by reading library books or looking at videos concerned with cities. The major requirements of cities should be noted and other important needs mentioned: housing; transportation; business and industry; waste management; parks and recreation; government; safety, health and emergency services; cultural and spiritual sites; and, yes, schools. Rather than turn this into a didactic exercise, wait for each group—

working independently—to come up with their own ideas. By the second half of a school year, even kindergartners have enough experience to contribute ideas. The discussions prior to making the city should also emphasize cooperation and the difference between doing a group project and an individual one. This is a wonderful opportunity for children to learn how decisions are made in the adult world.

In addition, this project can be a great way for a child to explore his or her environment. You can invite a fire or transportation department official, a landscaper, or a city planner to visit the classroom—or take a field trip to visit them. Visit a downtown, a park, a recycling center at a dump. Take a ride on mass transit or just explore streets.

Perhaps some of the children have traveled to other cities and have material to contribute, like photos or postcards. You might even take a look at

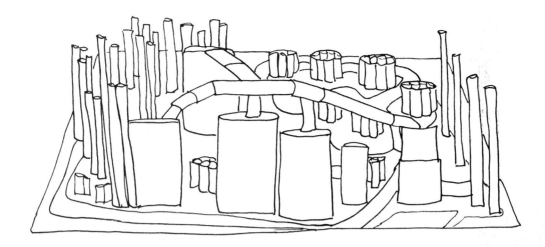

local history in preparation for this project. Joseph Campbell says you can tell what is important to a society by which buildings are tallest. Students might look into cities from their own ethnic heritage, via library books.

It is worth noting that the key elements—center, boundaries, and gateways—are found in cities and other structural sites of old all over the world. Today, the geomancy movement is studying ancient sites and methods of planning. Such material could be a launching point for planning a city. For instance, a group could use boundaries and gateways as a framework for its plans.

It is important not to overload the students with data. The simple elements mentioned above will connect students to basic principles that they can use to organize their own experience. That their center is a candy factory or a haunted house is not important. Making the decision as a group and planning a site that has parts related to a whole is.

Building the cities: The first session is for planning. The group meets around its base with pencils and erasers and plots out the major features of its city. Group members can check out the cylinder supply to see what they have to work with. There will be arguments, sometimes heated, and an adult should be supervising each group to point out how problems might be solved. The value of the practice at working together is incalculable.

One group may go all out on a single aspect—an exotic mass transit system, for example. Another may focus on cute little houses and parks. Some will want to start drawing the swings in the park or others will get involved in a fancy construction of their own. These children will need gentle reminders to work together in a sequential way. When they bypass each other and try to communicate through the adult, sometimes to complain behind the other's back, ask them to speak and listen to each other. They are usually able to work out the problem. Just as with adults, some will compromise more easily than others and a few may never want to compromise in any way. At that point, try diverting their attention to another part of the city, where something else may catch their fancy.

The second and third sessions are for arranging the cylinders and gluing them in place. Cylinders make great building units because they stand up on their own easily and they hold their shape with handling. They can be used alone or combined in interesting ways. Make sure the students can reach into the center of the city; working on the floor works well. The adult can now stay in the background, enjoying the wonderful conversations and being available to help in any way needed.

Painting the cities: The last sessions are pure fun, when each group paints its city. There is nothing as soothing as painting. Everyone will have settled down by now. The overly conscientious can relax and not worry about doing things wrong. The bosses can stop worrying about others doing things wrong. And the "detail" people can have a field day. The paint transforms the funky cardboard into a unified fantasy construction. Children may want to add small "junk" items to create three-dimensional details.

I don't hold any discussions after the cities are finished. They speak for themselves. Eventually, you can cut the cities up and each student can take his or her favorite part home.

APPLE DOLLS

TIME One 15- to 30-minute session for carving; a 2- to 3-month drying time; one 15-minute session for finishing a simple doll

MATERIALS Round, firm, not-too-ripe apples

Vegetable peelers

Butter knives and pumpkin carvers for young children; older children may use sharper carving tools when supervised

Wooden skewers

Drying stand: A piece of wood or sturdy cardboard with skewer-sized holes

Toothpicks

Newspapers

Optional: Beans, small stones, yarn, shells, feathers, fabric, etc.

Apple and nut dolls are the only indigenous American dolls. Early settlers learned this craft from Native Americans whose carved, dried heads were finished simply with a cloth "blanket," feathers, and beads.

DOING IT Spread newspapers on a table. Adults should peel the apples for younger children. Older children can peel their own, and may even want to leave some of the peel as a part of the design.

This is a "think before you do" project. If you start cutting without thinking, you may end up with nothing but a core! Suggest that the children feel their faces. What areas are "hills" and what are "valleys?" Have them look at the apple and decide which side is the front. Once this is done, they must decide where the nose will go. (They can trace the shape with a toothpick.) Carve eye sockets on either side of the nose. Eyes can be round, triangular, or almond-shaped; they can be carved deeply (which tends to make the face look mad or sad), or carved around, leaving "pop eyes" (which may look comical). When you have carved the eye-

sockets, the nose area will be left standing out. Now carve the area under the nose, around the lips, and the place under the lips so the chin will stick out. You can also carve ears, eyebrows, hair dimples, and wrinkles. Beans, beads, and the like can be stuck into the apple; the fruit will shrink around them and hold them in place. Stick the apple head onto a skewer and set the skewer in the piece of wood with skewer-sized holes or in the cardboard with holes. If drying a group of apples, do not let them touch each other or anything else. Put them in a warm place, out of direct sunlight, but where the children can watch them shrink. They should be warned that an apple can shrink to less than half its original size when completely dry. Its hard to predict what the final results will be, but it certainly is fun to watch the process. In the early drying stages, some mold may form, adding interesting color. Surprisingly enough, very few apples will rot completely. Once dried, apple heads may last for years.

Dried heads may be finished into dolls in the original manner with a "blanket" tied around the skewer, a headband, and decorations of choice.

CONCLUSION

The Summertime Arts & Crafts Workshop has succeeded and remained viable for several years mainly because of three factors: It is a program that people want and need; it has been able to secure consistent funding; and it was based on the sound educational model I adopted from Mike McBride's Open Alternative School class.

As an artist and a parent, I was alarmed at the lack of art in public school. Almost all the other parents I knew felt the same way. That strong feeling, combined with a spirit of experimentation, prompted me to seek financial support for a small art workshop to be held during the summer of 1984. I asked the permission of three teachers at the school where I worked as an aide to send home a brief survey for parents. I incorporated the overwhelmingly positive results into a proposal. (Proposals should be heartfelt and must contain a projected budget before any requests can be made. The original proposal has been updated annually and is combined with an annual report.)

I had decided that, if I was able to raise a certain modest sum of money by a certain date, I would go forward. Starting close to home, I had luck with a savings and loan company, a dairy, a small department store, a small but successful manufacturer, and a service club. I began to realize that there are sincere people willing to donate funds for children's projects and that giving is a tradition that runs deep in our country.

A combination of luck, timing, and hard work resulted in the program becoming officially nonprofit soon after the first summer. The luck came when Alice Smith, secretary of the Smith Family Foundation (a small, nonprofit corporation dedicated to health and education), waited in line to enroll her children. After she learned about the program's funding needs, she brought the project proposal to her board. The board voted to adopt the proposal because the goals it outlined were in line with the stated purpose of the foundation. Acquiring nonprofit status is essential, but doing this on one's own is time-consuming and expensive. Joining with an already-established nonprofit is a viable alternative for a small or temporary program. The Summertime Arts & Crafts Workshop has since moved on to become part of the recently formed Sebastopol Center for the Arts. The increased establishment of local arts centers is a heartening development, and such centers are certainly the logical place to start if a program you envision needs funding.

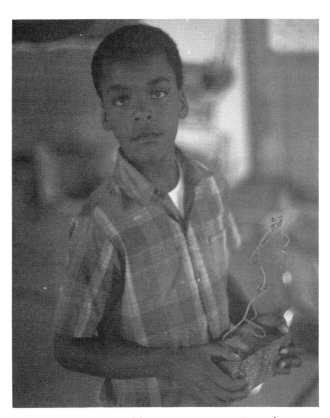

Byron Whitlock invented his own project, a wire sculpture, from materials left at our workshop by the telephone company.

Over the years, the workshop budget has increased to twenty-five times that of that first summer. Funding sources are varied. The smaller, local businesses and the service clubs—Rotary, Kiwanis—are still an important source of support. We have added larger corporations with local ties; some have special programs when children of employees are involved.

Though I find that fund-raising from businesses is far less complicated than from foundations, I have also sought and received several grants. The grant-making world is a formal and highly organized one. There are three kinds of foundations: private, corporate, and community. Nonprofit status is required for application to foundations. Without too much effort, it is possible to find the information needed to apply. Some states may have Foundation Centers (resource centers for grant seekers) in one of their larger cities. Communities with volunteer organizations and universities offer grant-writing workshops on a regular basis, and libraries have source books on foundations in their reference sections.

Another part of the summer workshop's funding comes from the city of Sebastopol. Cities fund non-profit programs by means of local taxes. It is not a good idea to become too dependent on this source, which may fluctuate, but city funding gives a major boost to a program's credibility and further ability to raise funds. My small city has a five-member council and a city manager. The manager and the head commissioner of the Parks and Recreation Department (once again, through his children) became aware of the workshop and helped me learn the process of requesting city funds. This requires a yearly request, including a formal appearance before the council to provide information and answer questions. I had never imagined myself doing such things but somehow made it through with much support from parents.

Student fees constitute about one third of our revenue. Although I was forced to give up my original dream of a free program, we have remained accessible by means of a sliding fee scale and scholarships. A suggested fee is included with our registration material, and parents pay on the honor system. Since average fees received have increased over the years, I feel the fee system is working well.

The keys to fund-raising, in my opinion, are a good program and good manners. One of our local, long-time supporters told me that he really appreciated our annual report and proposal because it showed respect for him and the demands on his business. Prompt thank-you letters (as personal as is possible) are also important. A good book for further research is Kim Klein's *Fund-raising for Social Change.*

Besides there being a need for a children's art program, I was successful in fund-raising because I had a definite plan for using the funds, and the plan was based on experience and knowledge. While the debate over public education drones on, individual parents and educators have sought a variety of solutions to school reform from within. In 1977, the first Open Alternative School (OAS) class was established (under California's Dunlap Bill) by such a group of parents along with teacher Mike McBride and with the permission of the school board. The alternative school movement has been active and effective nationally for over twenty years (see *Public Schools of Choice,* by Mario Fantini).

The "open classroom" alternative style of education was initiated in England. This model was studied there and adopted in the sixties by educators in the United States. I became especially interested in the subject when my eldest son entered kindergarten, and my investigation was prompted by my belief in and concern about public education. By the time my husband and I enrolled our younger son in Mike's class in 1981, the open-style structure was well-defined, refined, and imbued with his personal innovations. I became active as a parent volunteer in art; later I was a classroom aide. I became a long-term substitute teacher in the OAS classroom after acquiring a special temporary elementary credential. Although I never attended educational courses (my credential is for teaching in a community college), as a parent in the classroom I learned classroom techniques firsthand by observing an exemplary, experienced, and creative teacher. The first Summertime Art & Crafts Workshop classes took place in an OAS classroom where there were large work tables instead of individual

desks and other features that lent themselves to an art program. The structural elements of OAS that I incorporated into the workshop were as follows:

- Parent involvement inside and outside the classroom
- Mixed-age student group
- Learning centers
- Class meetings
- Choices for students and an emphasis on decision making.

Judging from the yearly evaluations of the program, these elements contribute very much to the program's success. This is not the only way to structure a program. The point is that I knew how it worked and I was devoted to the rationale behind its existence.

The administration of a successful children's program must be based on a sound structure of experience, knowledge, and integrity. Artists often make outstanding teachers of young people, but are rarely credentialed. Individuals must use their common sense and intuition to assess teachers and leaders of children's programs. Parents are all too often intimidated by their own past experiences at school to speak when they know in their hearts what they want for their children.

It is my hope that parents will take heart in my experiences and realize that they, as parents, do have considerable power as advocates for their children. Even parents who work full-time can elect and communicate with their local school board representatives; keep abreast of readings concerning education, which are available at the public library; and make periodic visits to their child's classroom. At the community level, should they wish to initiate a needed program (be it in art, sports, or language), they should be encouraged to find that there are funds available, even in trying times, from responsible individuals and groups who will donate out of the sheer love of children and the desire for ensuring the future of our society. Let us reverse the trend that Ivan Illich described when he wrote: "Surreptitiously, reliance on institutional process has replaced dependence on personal good will."

BIBLIOGRAPHY

REFERENCES, ART

Albright, Thomas. *Art in the San Francisco Bay Area.* University of California Press, Berkeley, 1985.

Allison, Linda and Allison, Stella. *Rags.* Clarkson N. Potter, New York, 1979.

Arnheim, Rudolf. *Art and Visual Perception.* University of California Press, Berkeley, 1960.

Baird, Bil. *The Art of the Puppet.* Ridge Press, New York, 1973.

Beardsley, John, and Livingston, Jane. *Black Folk Art in America.* University of Mississippi Press, Jackson, 1982.

Berensohn, Paulus. *Finding One's Way With Clay.* Simon & Schuster, New York, 1980.

Berrin, Kathleen, editor. *Art of the Huichol Indians.* Harry N. Abrams, New York, 1979.

Cheneviere, Alain. *Vanishing Tribes.* Doubleday & Co., New York, 1987.

Cordry, Donald. *Mexican Masks.* University of Texas Press, Austin, 1980.

Courtney-Clarke, Margaret. *African Canvas.* Rizzoli International Publications, New York, 1990.

Edwards, Betty. *Drawing on the Right Side of the Brain.* Jeremy P. Tarcher, Los Angeles, 1989.

Ekiguchi, Kunio. *Origami for Christmas.* Kodansha International Press, Tokyo, 1983.

Feder, Norman. *American Indian Art.* Harry N. Abrams, New York, 1973.

Fisher, Angela. *Africa Adorned.* Harry N. Abrams, New York, 1984.

Flack, Audrey. *Audrey Flack on Painting.* Harry N. Abrams, New York, 1985.

Folch, Alberto, and Serra, Eudald. *The Art of Papua and New Guinea.* Rizzoli Press, New York, 1977.

Harter, Jim, Ed., *Animals: 1,419 Copyright-Free Illustrations of Mammals, Birds, Fish, Insects, Etc.* Dover Publications, New York, 1985.

Hopkins, Henry T. *California Painters: New Work.* Chronicle Books, San Francisco, 1989.

Huet, Michel. *The Dance, Art, and Ritual of Africa.* Pantheon Books, New York, 1978.

Itten, Johannes. *The Elements of Color.* Van Nostrand Reinhold Co., New York, 1970.

Jones, Caroline A. *Manuel Neri Plasters.* San Francisco Museum of Modern Art, San Francisco, 1989.

Koike, Kazuko and Tanaka, Ikko. *Japan Color.* Chronicle Books, San Francisco, 1982.

Laporte, Dominique. *Christo.* Pantheon Books, New York, 1986.

Lindstrom, Miriam. *Children's Art.* University of California Press, Berkeley, 1957.

Longstreet, Stephen. *A Treasury of the World's Great Prints.* Simon & Schuster, New York, 1961.

Mayer, Ralph. *The Artist's Handbook of Materials and Techniques,* 4th ed. Viking Penguin, New York, 1985.

Mendelowitz, Daniel M. *Drawing*. Holt, Rinehart and Winston, New York, 1967.

Ozenfant. *Foundations of Modern Art*. Dover Publications, New York, 1952.

Page, Suzanne and Page, Jake. *Hopi*. Harry N. Abrams, New York, 1986.

Pomar, Maria Teresa. *El Dia de los Muertos*. Fort Worth Museum of Art, Fort Worth, 1987.

Seiberling, Frank. *Looking into Art*. Holt, Rinehart and Winston, New York, 1987.

Smith, Ray. *The Artist's Handbook*. Alfred A. Knopf, New York, 1987.

Stern, Harold P. *Birds, Beasts, Blossoms, and Bugs: The Nature of Japan*. Harry N. Abrams, New York, 1976.

Vogel, Susan, and N'Diaye, Francine. *African Masterpieces from the Musée de l'Homme*. The Center for African Arts, New York, and Harry N. Abrams, New York, 1985.

Walking Turtle, Eagle. *Keepers of the Fire*. Bear and Co., Santa Fe, 1987.

Wechsler, Herman J. *Great Prints and Printmakers*. Harry N. Abrams, and N. V., Bentveld, The Netherlands.

White, John. *The Birth and Rebirth of Pictorial Space*. Faber and Faber, London, 1957.

REFERENCES, EDUCATION AND OTHER TOPICS OF INTEREST

Armstrong, Thomas. *In Their Own Way*. Jeremy P. Tarcher, Los Angeles, 1987.

Crowley, Aleister. *A Handbook of Geomancy*. Holmes Publishers, Oakland, California, 1989.

Decker, Larry E., and Schoeny, Donna Hager. *Community, Educational, and Social Impact Perspectives*. University of Virginia Printing Office, Charlottesville, 1983.

Fantini, Mario. *Public Schools of Choice*. Simon & Schuster, New York, 1973.

Fuller, Buckminster. *Critical Path*. St. Martin's Press, New York, 1981.

Gattegno, Caleb. *What We Owe Children*. Outerbridge & Dienstfrey, New York, 1970.

Holt, John. *How Children Learn*, rev. ed. Delta/Seymour Lawrence, New York, 1983.

————, *How Children Fail*, rev. ed. Delta/Seymour Lawrence, New York, 1983.

Illich, Ivan. *Deschooling Society*. Harper & Row, New York, 1971.

Klein, Kim. *Fund-raising for Social Change*. Chardon Press, Inverness, California, 1988.

Pennick, Nigel. *The Ancient Science of Geomancy: Living with the Earth*. CRCS Publications, Sebastopol, California, 1987.

Read, Herbert. *Education Through Art*. Random House, New York, 1956.

Reimer, Everett. *School Is Dead*. Doubleday & Co., New York, 1971.

Report of the School Readiness Task Force. *Here They Come: Ready or Not*. California State Department of Education, Sacramento, 1988.

Silberman, Charles E., ed. *The Open Classroom Reader*. Random House, New York, 1973.

INDEX